Niagara Falls Ontario Book 3 in Colour Photos, Saving Our History One Photo at a Time

Photography by Barbara Raué
©2021

Series Name: Cruising Ontario

Book Niagara Falls Book 3

Cover photo: 21 Bowen Road, Chippawa, Page 69

©2021 All the photos in this book have been taken with my cameras. I own the rights to them.

Table of Contents

Jepson Street	Page 5
McRae Street	Page 14
Second Avenue	Page 15
Armoury Street	Page 19
Kitchener Street	Page 20
Hunter Street	Page 21
Walnut Street	Page 22
Victoria Avenue	Page 23
Terrace Avenue	Page 26
Church's Lane	Page 29
Portage Road	Page 31
St. Paul Avenue	Page 36
St. Patrick Avenue	Page 41
Chippawa	Page 57
Bridgewater Street	
Main Street	
Niagara Parkway	
Bowen Road	

Niagara Falls Ontario is located along the Niagara Gorge on the western bank of the Niagara River, which flows from Lake Erie to Lake Ontario. The Niagara River flows over Niagara Falls at this location and creates a natural spectacle that attracts millions of tourists each year. Niagara Falls is about 130 kilometers (81 miles) by road from Toronto, which is across Lake Ontario to the north.

Tourism started in the early nineteenth century. The falls became known as a natural wonder, due in part to paintings by prominent American artists such as Albert Bierstadt. Niagara Falls is the self-proclaimed "honeymoon capital of the world."

With a plentiful and inexpensive source of hydroelectric power from the waterfalls, many electro-chemical and electro-metallurgical industries located there in the early to mid-20th century.

By 1792-94, a village grew up near Fort Chippawa on Chippawa Creek near the end of the new portage road from Queenston. In 1793, the creek was renamed the Welland River. The village was largely destroyed 1812-14 when the British and American forces fought for control of the Welland River. Portage traffic revived after the war and continued until Chippawa became an outlet for the original Welland Canal from 1829 to 1833. The first horse-powered railway in Upper Canada was built to Niagara Falls in 1837-39.

Precipitated by the opening of the Welland Canal in 1829, by the 1840s, Chippawa was a thriving town. A wide variety of business establishments were located around Cummington Square. Chippawa amalgamated with the City of Niagara Falls in 1970.

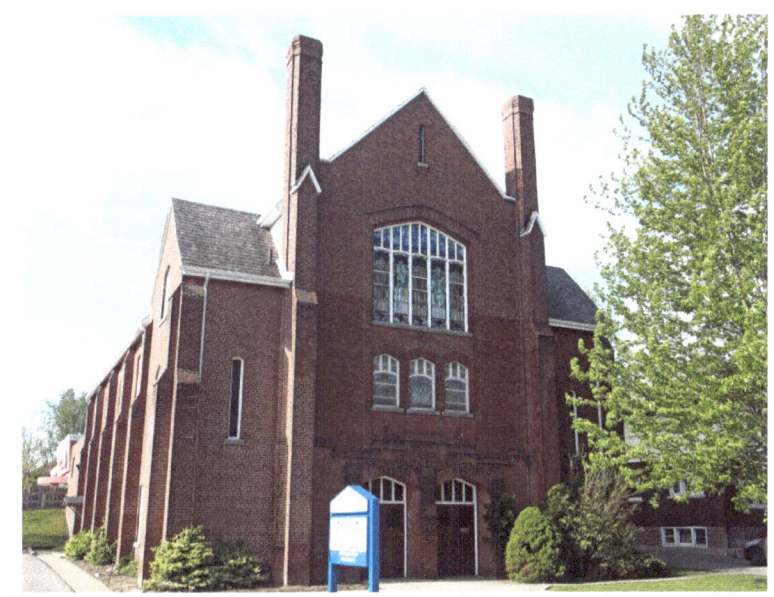

4878 Jepson Street – Faith Fellowship Christian Reformed Church

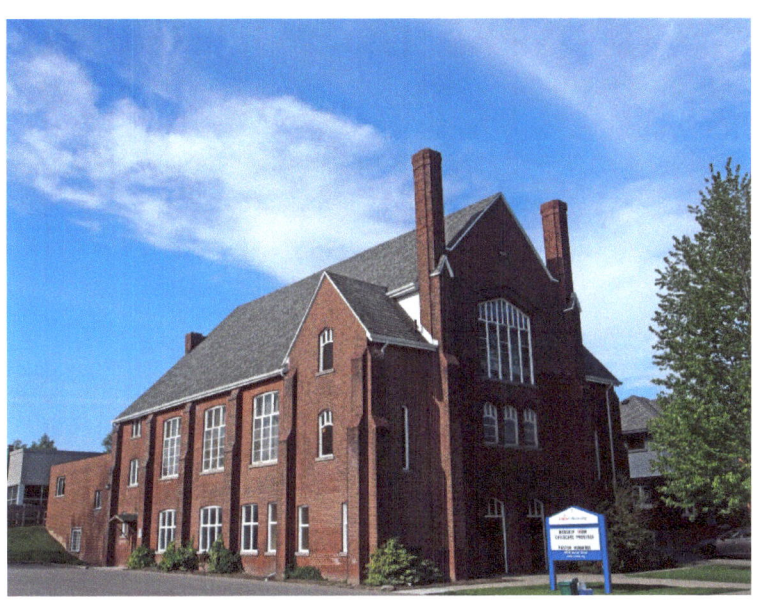

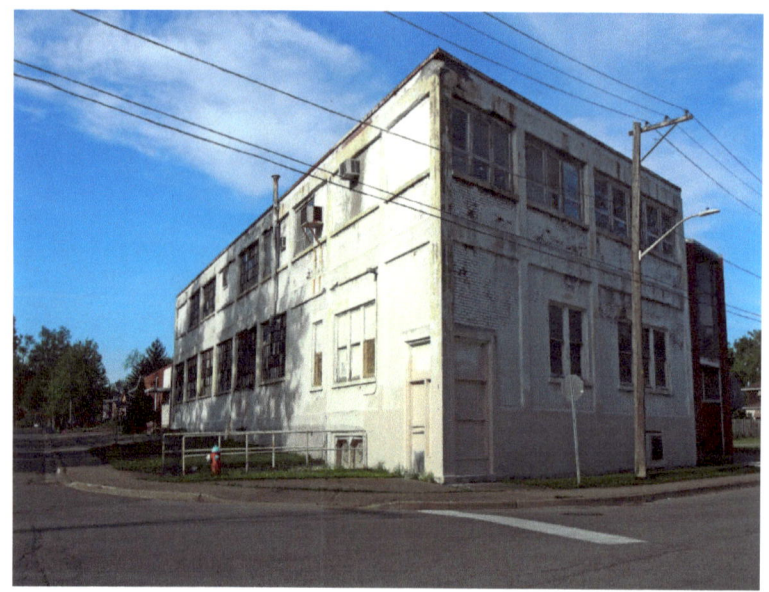

Jepson Street

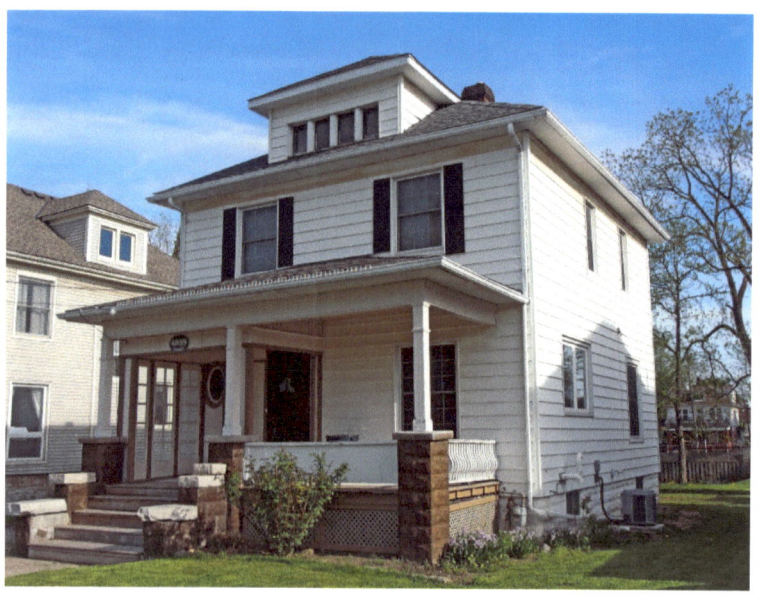

4859 Jepson Street

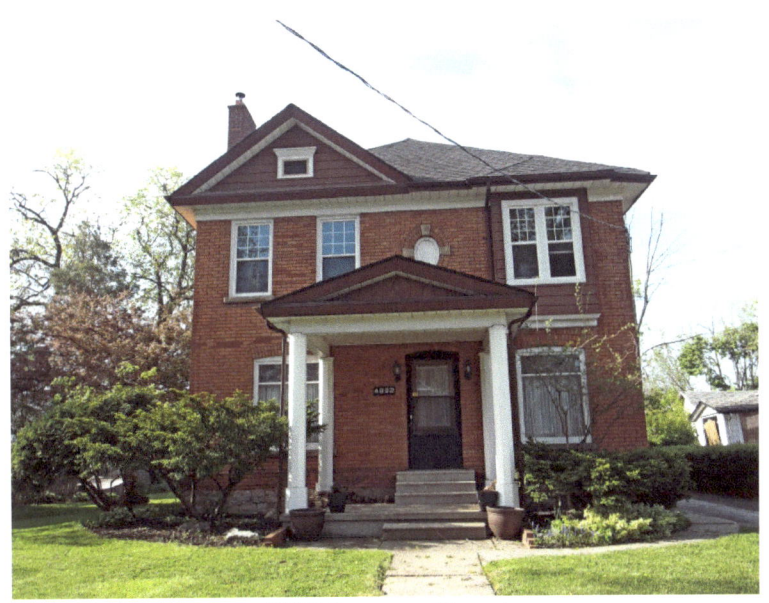

4892 Jepson Street

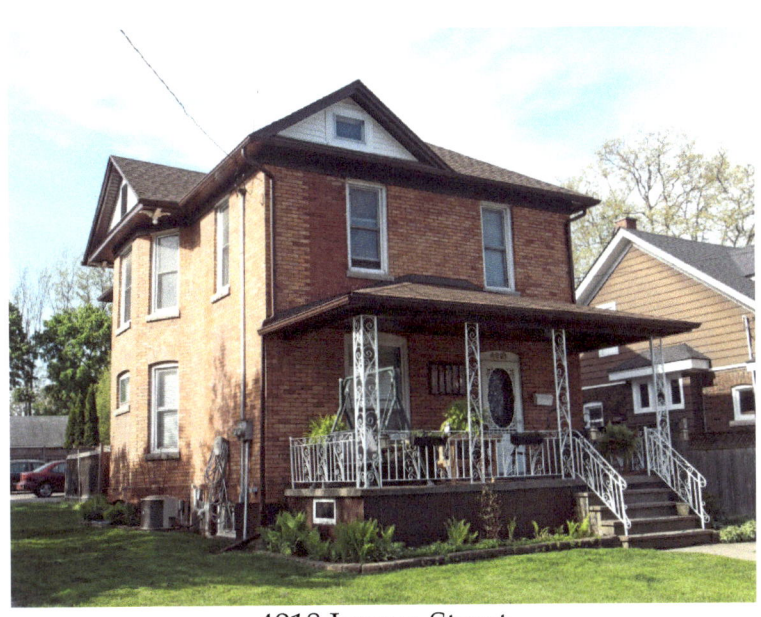

4918 Jepson Street

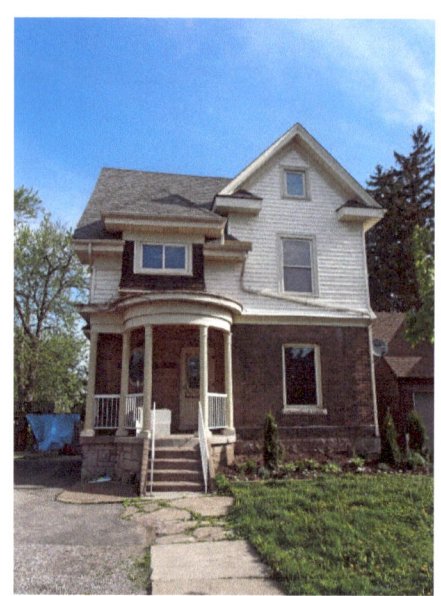

4905 Jepson Street

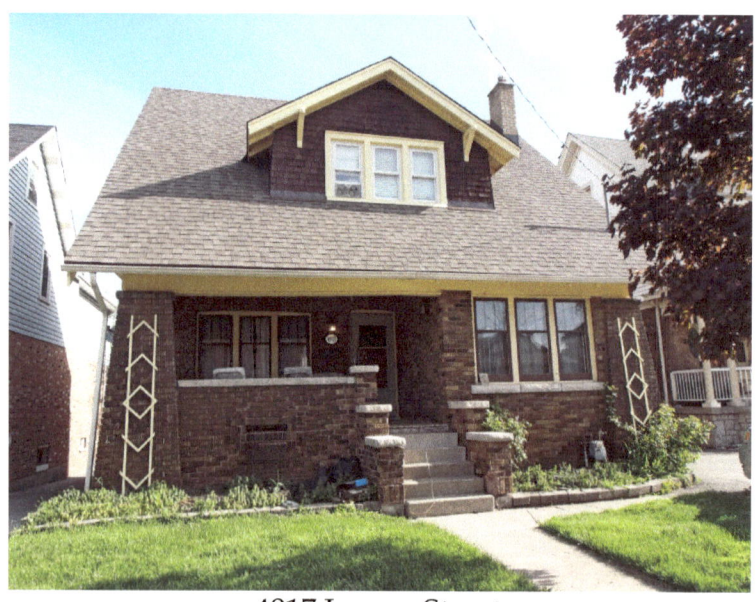

4917 Jepson Street

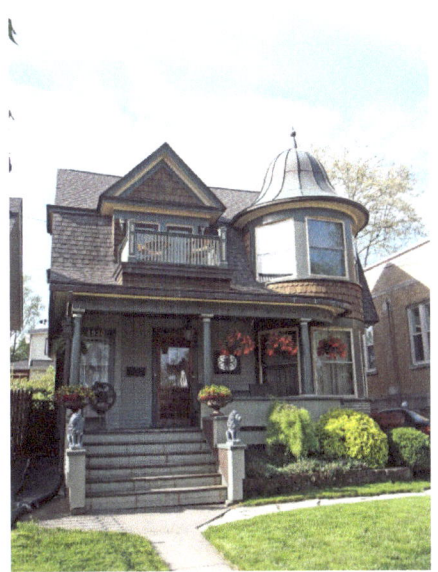

4930 Jepson Street

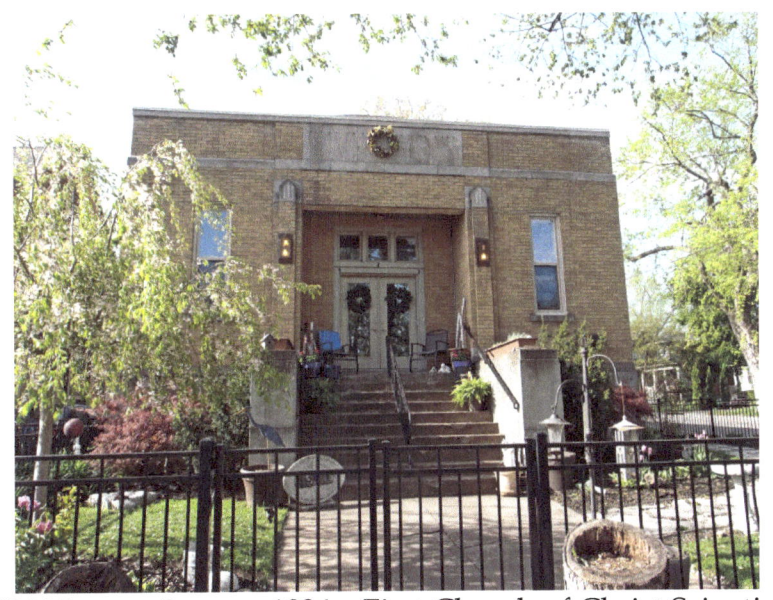

4940 Jepson Street – 1934 – First Church of Christ Scientist

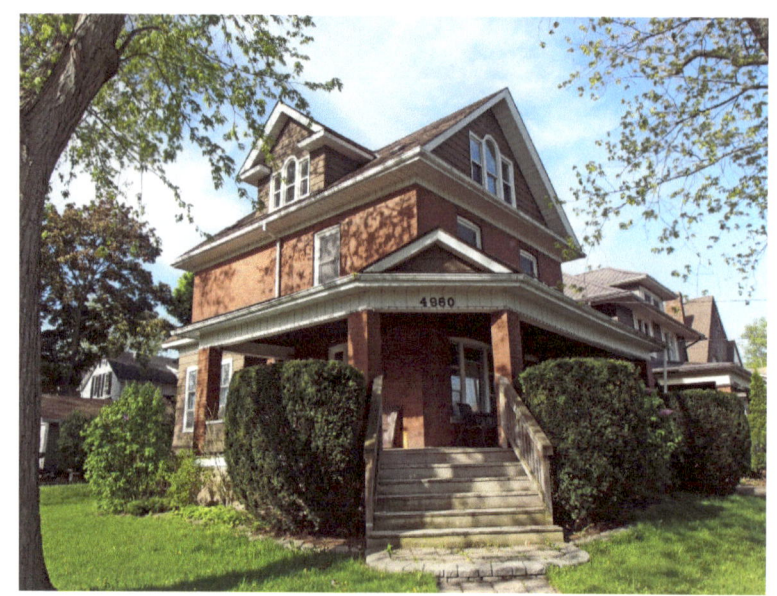

4960 Jepson Street

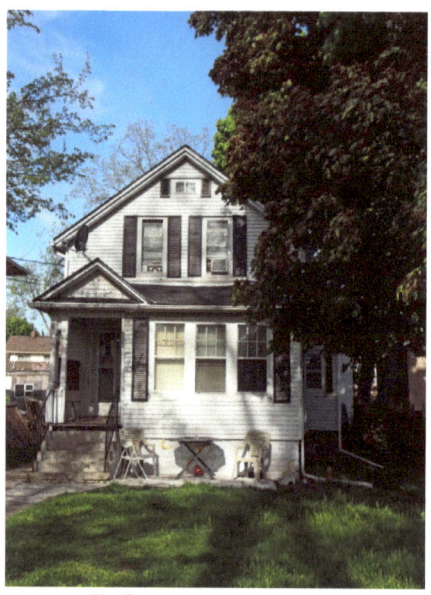

5127 Jepson Street

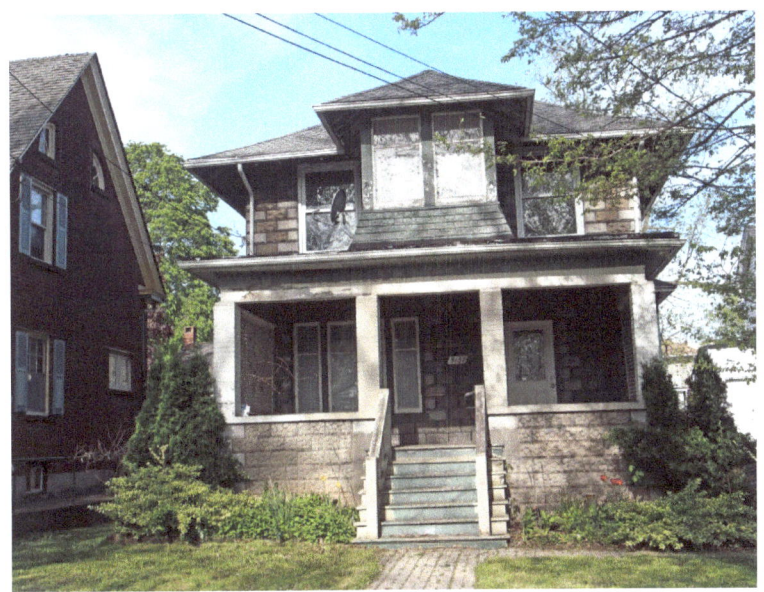

5137 Jepson Street

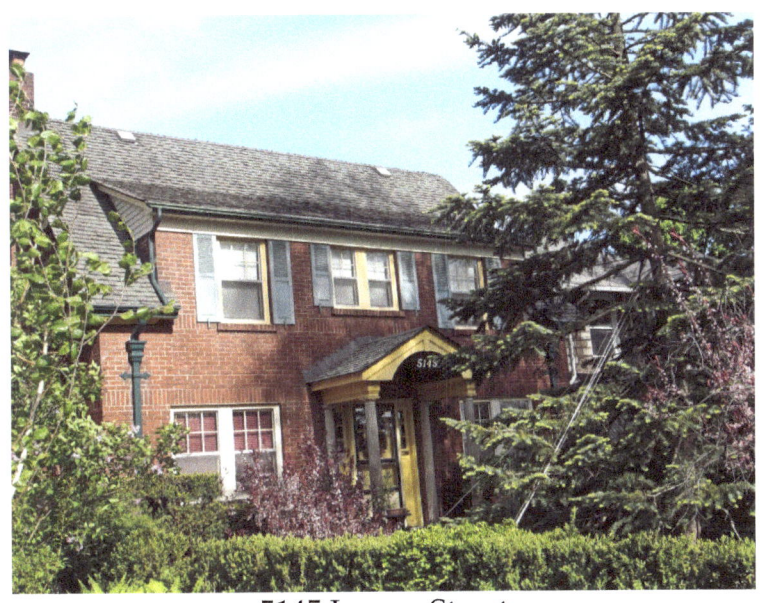

5145 Jepson Street

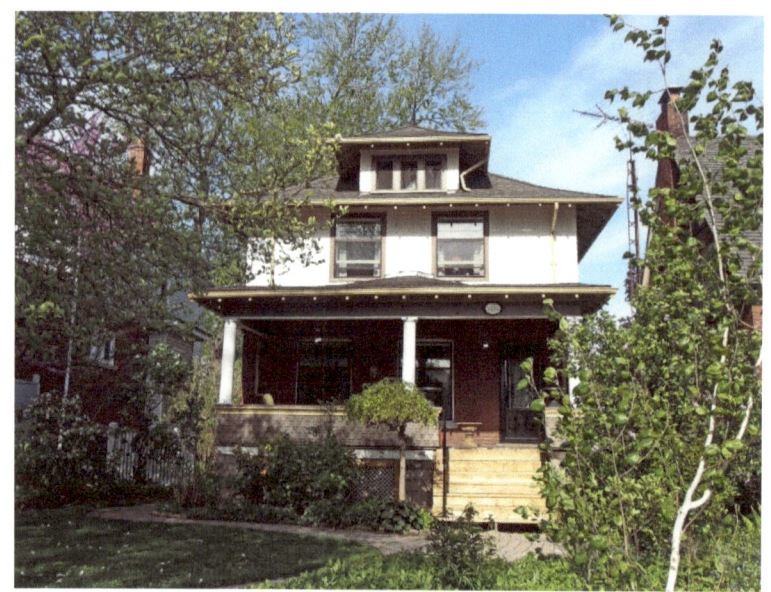
5151 Jepson Street

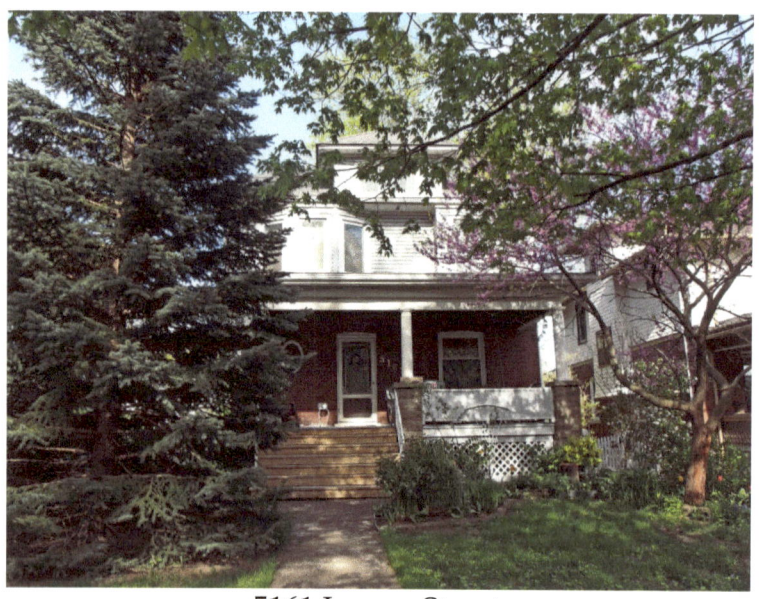
5161 Jepson Street

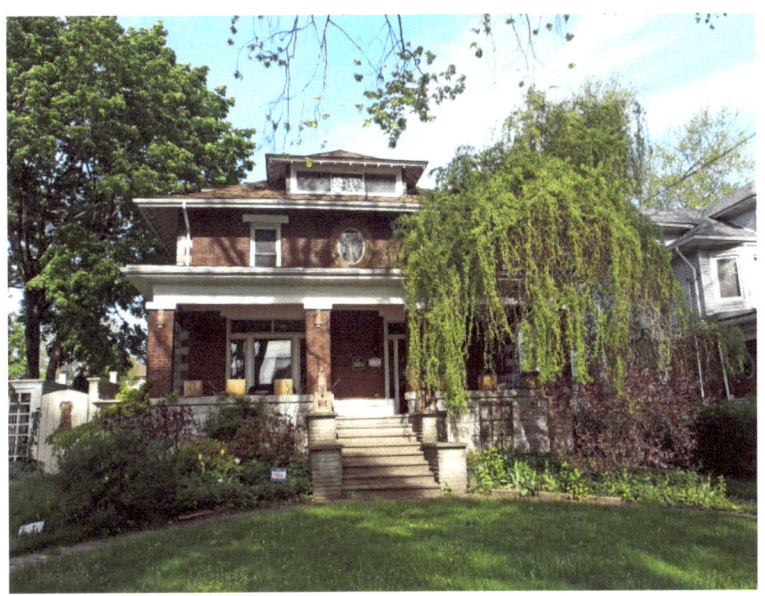

5171 Jepson Street

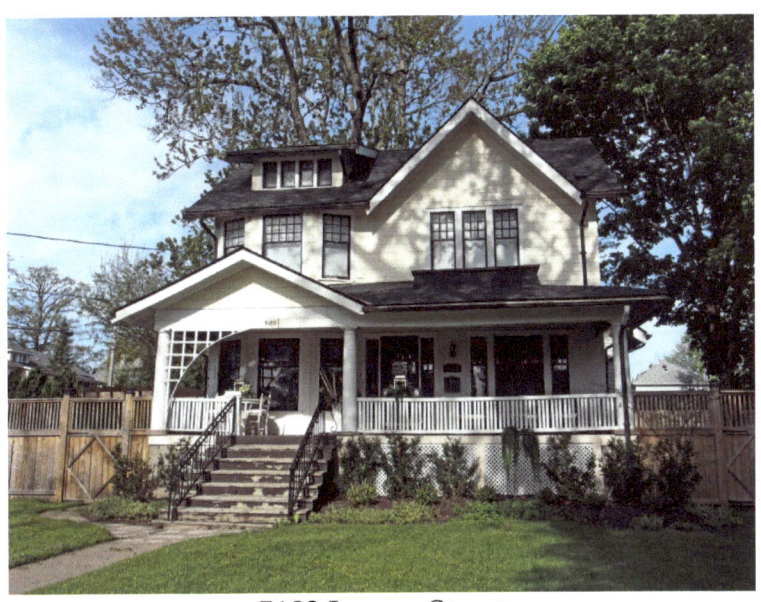

5183 Jepson Street

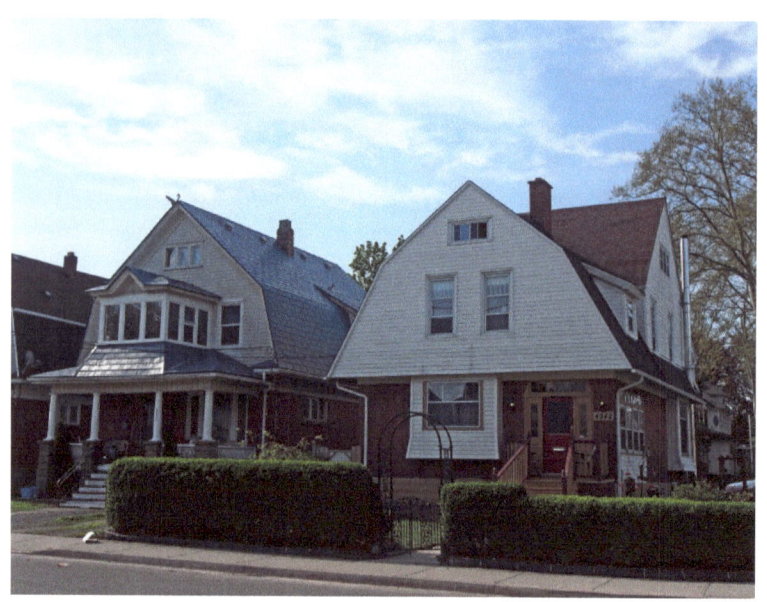

4934 and 4942 McRae Street

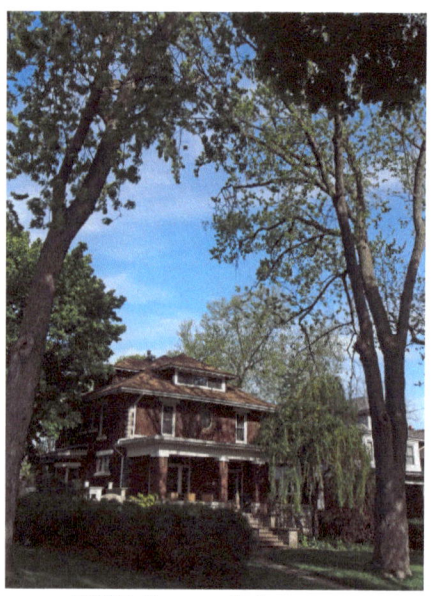

5171 Second Avenue

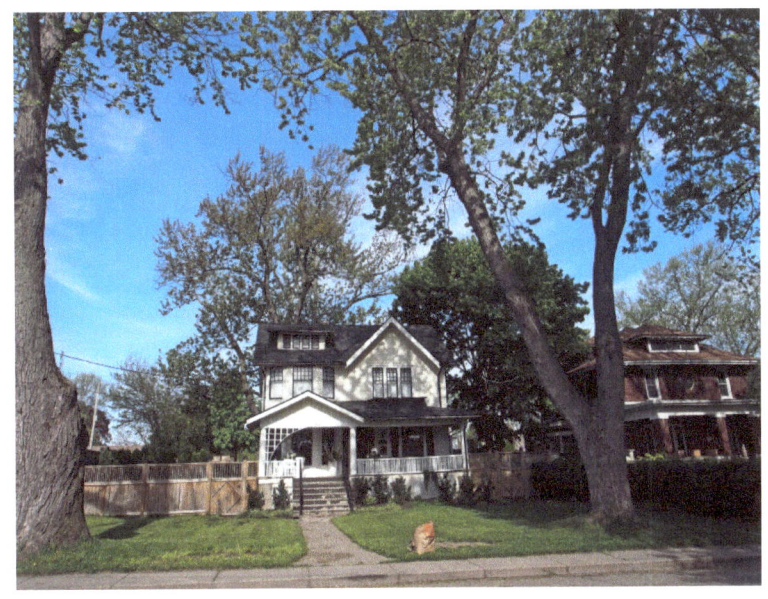

5183 Second Avenue – c. 1880s – trees planted at this time

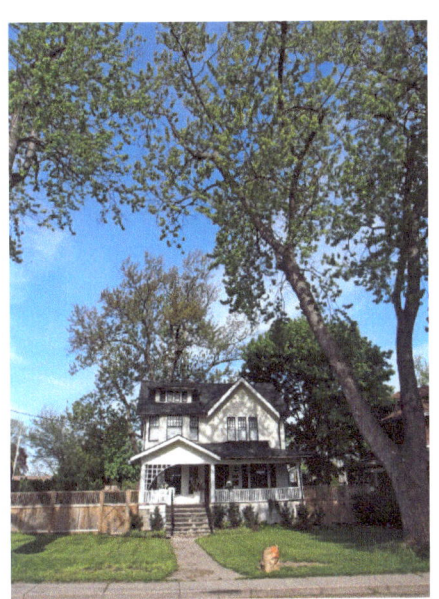
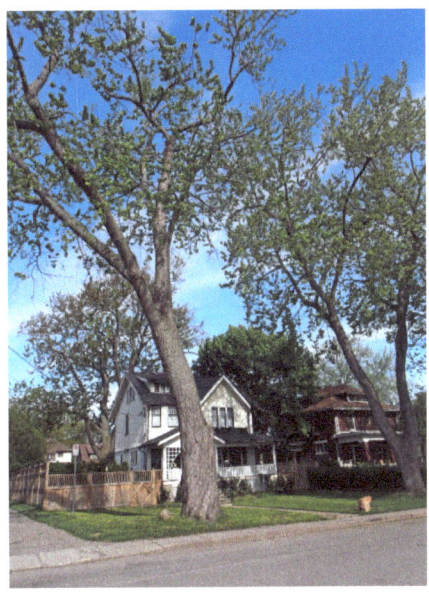

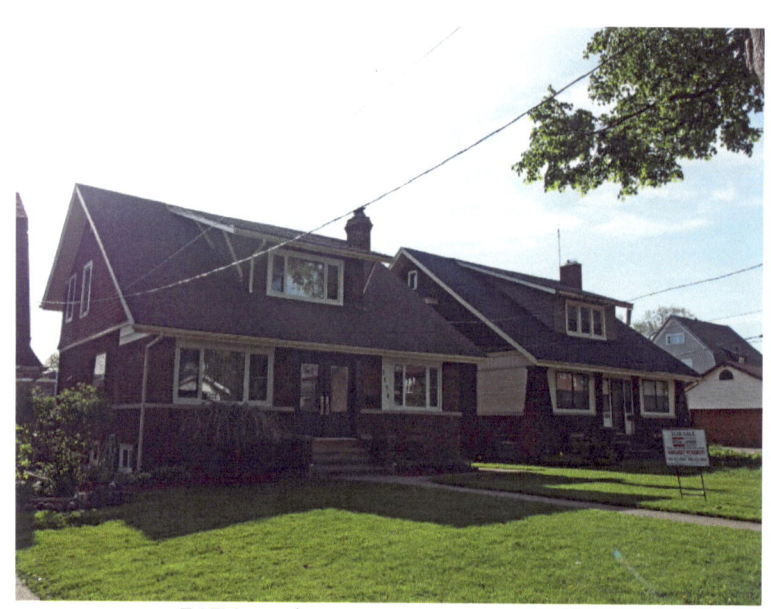

5176 and 5184 Second Avenue

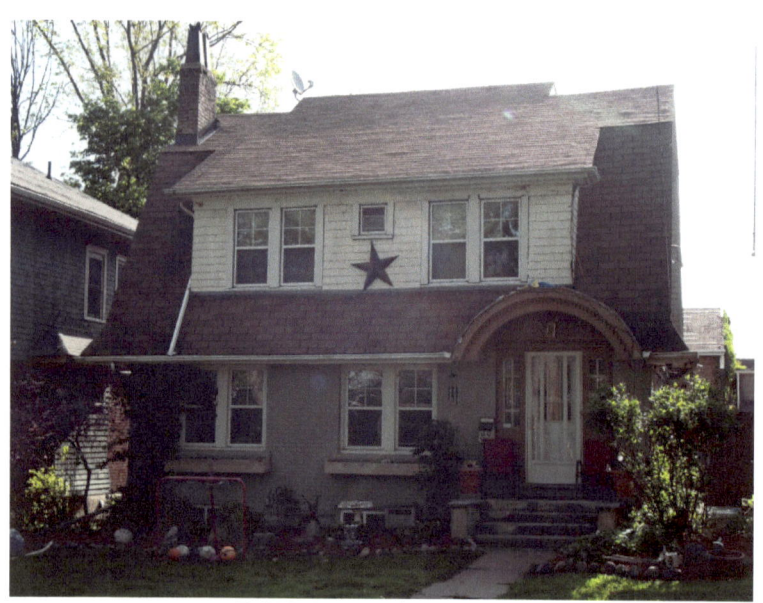

5170 Second Avenue

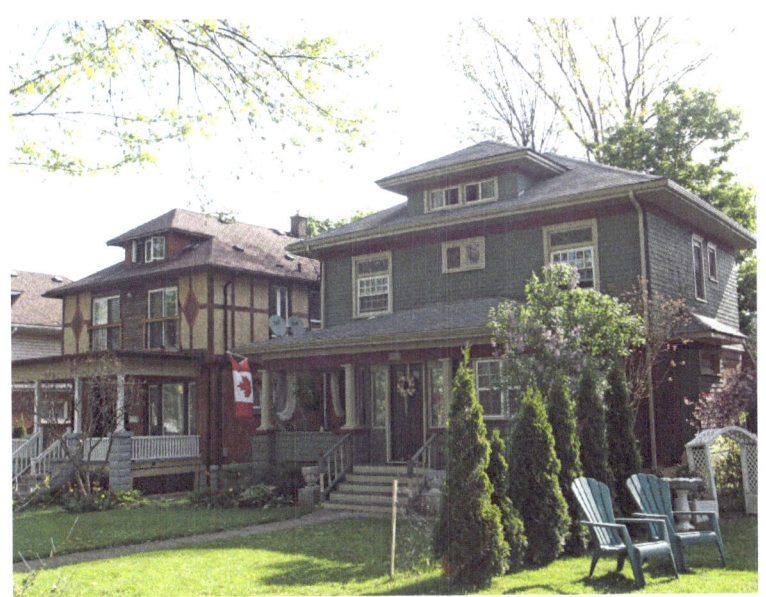

5160 Second Avenue

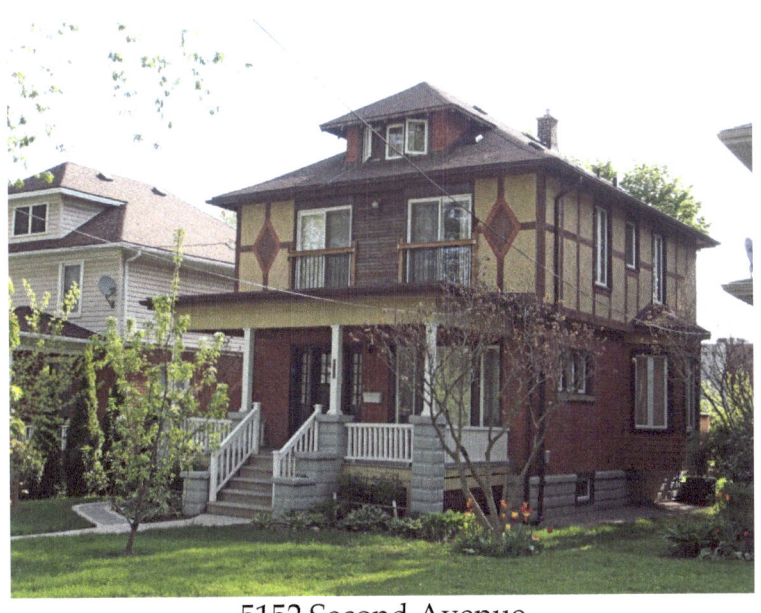

5152 Second Avenue

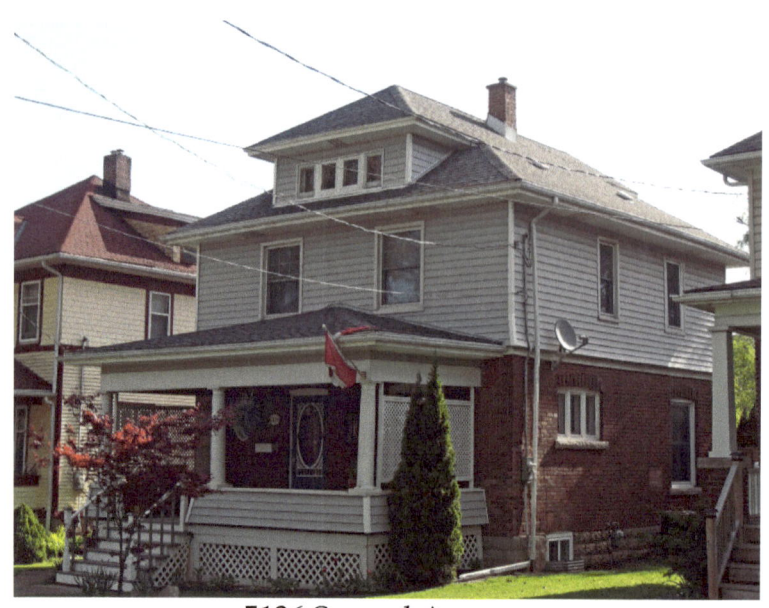

5136 Second Avenue

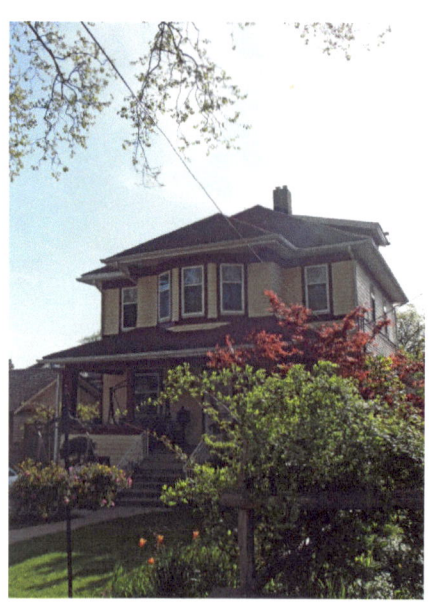

5128 Second Avenue

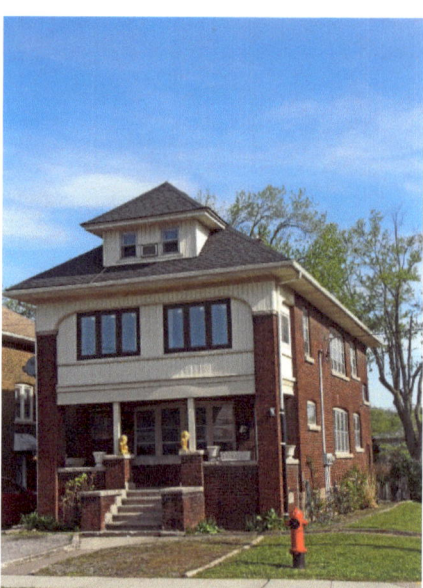

Armoury Street

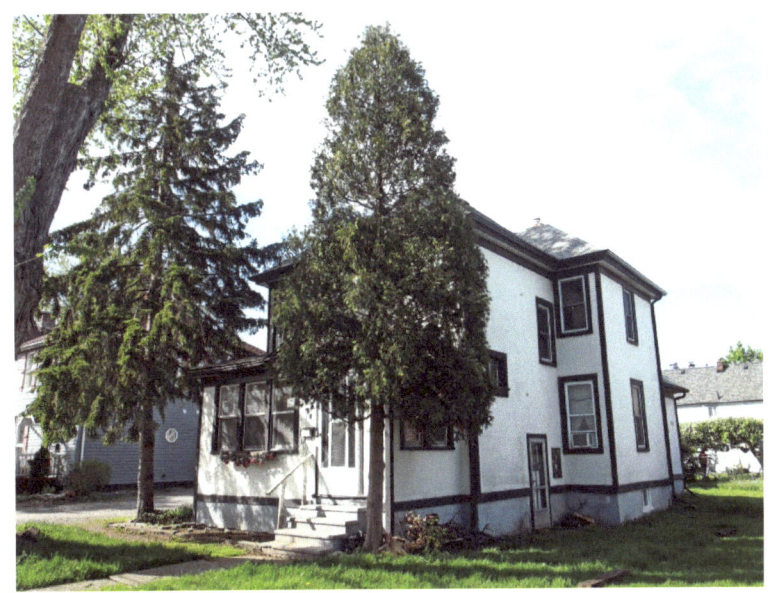

4910 Hunter Street

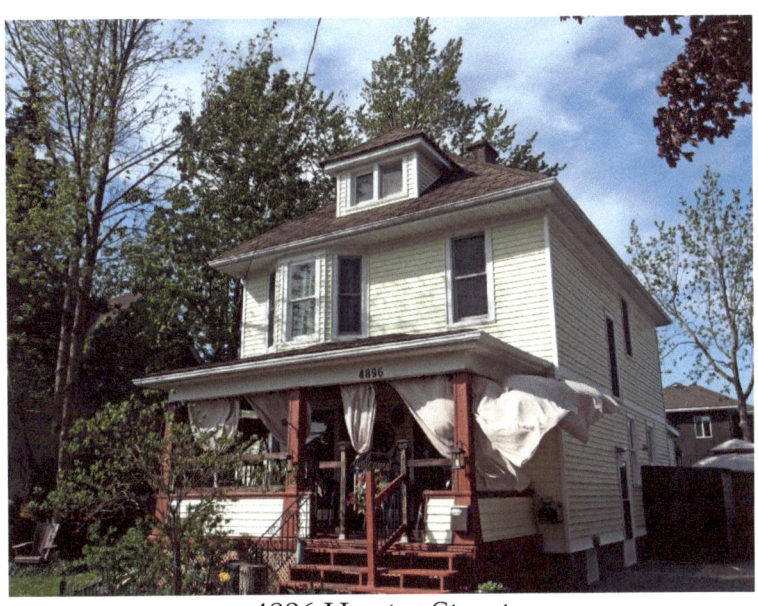

4896 Hunter Street

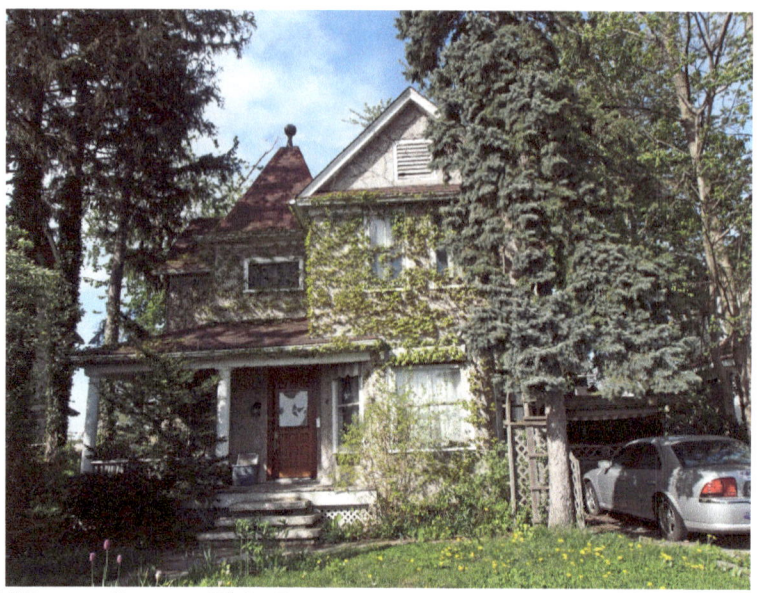

4888 Hunter Street – This Queen Anne Revival style house was originally covered in clapboard and later with stucco. The square front tower is topped with a peaked roof and round pommel-like copper finial. Every other floor joist is a half log and the foundation walls appear to be earth and rubble.

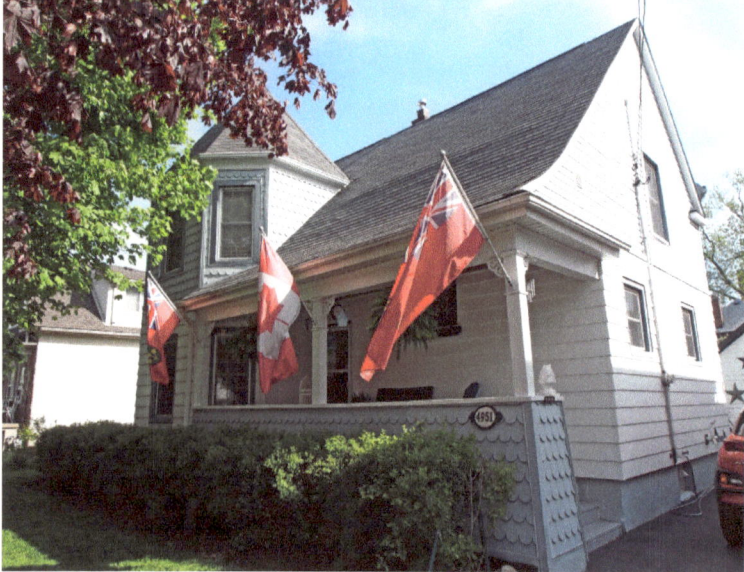

4951 Walnut Street

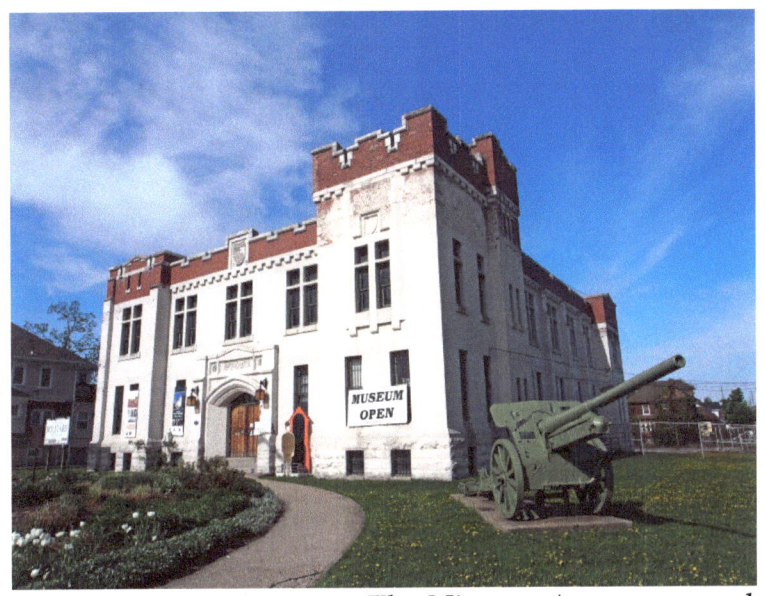

5049 Victoria Avenue - The Niagara Armoury was built in 1911 in the style of a late medieval fortress. It features simulated defense towers at the corners, a crenellated parapet and a massive front entrance formed by a Tudor Gothic arch. The red brick façade has limestone detailing such as windowsills surrounds capping and corbels now covered by paint.

It was designed by T. W. Fuller, a government military architect and son of Thomas Fuller who designed the old Post Office (SEE DP.9). It was one of 11 armories built during a period of reform and expansion in the Canadian Militia (1896-1911) and was a recruitment and training center during the First World War.

The building now houses the Niagara Military Museum.

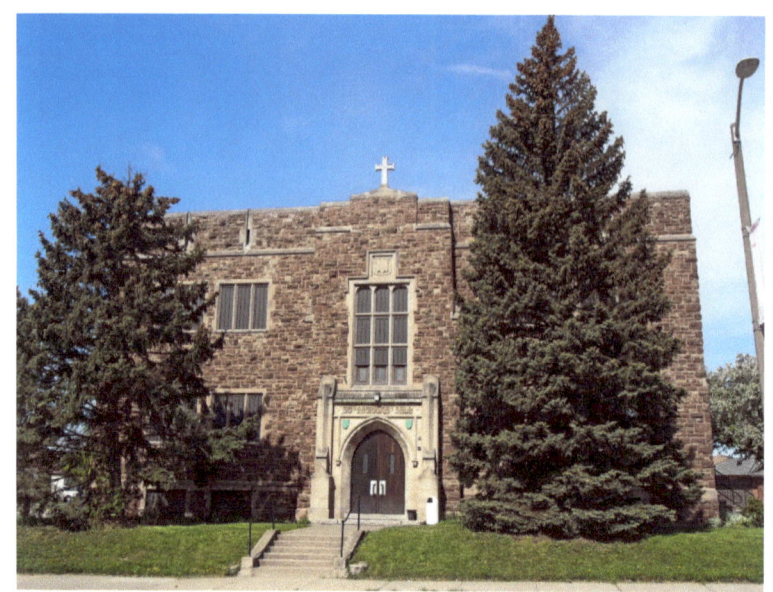
4673 Victoria Avenue – St. Patrick's Hall

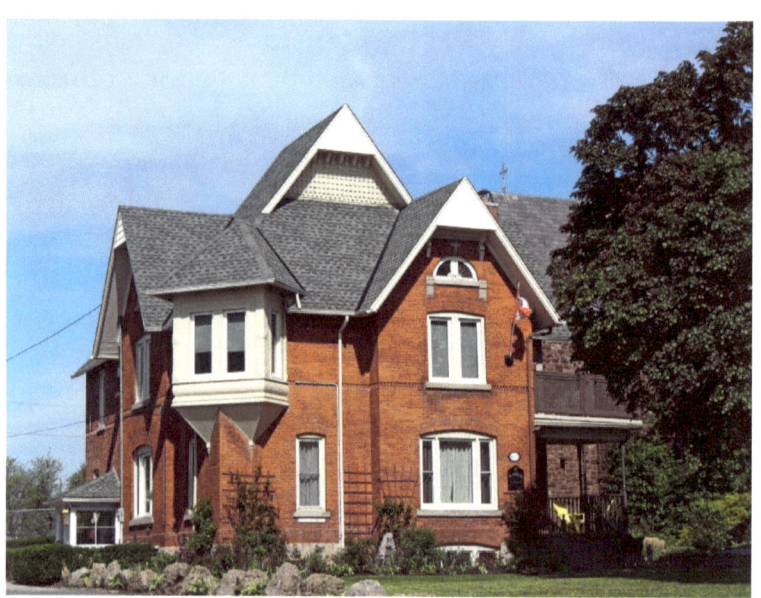
4673 Victoria Avenue – St. Patrick's Rectory

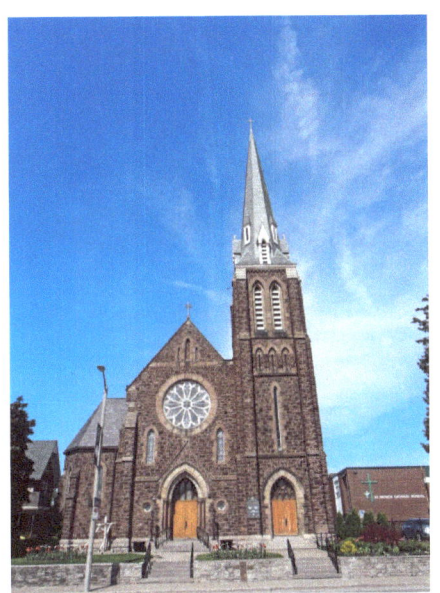 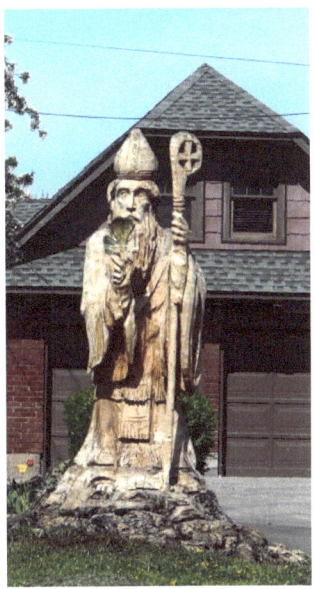

4673 Victoria Avenue – The red sandstone masonry of St. Patrick's Roman Catholic Church was laid by George Seales and the carpentry done by Waugh and Robertson. The most prominent features of its Gothic styling are the high, octagonal spire and large rose window on the east gable end. The original slate tile roof was replaced in 1995. The rectory to the south was built c.1897-99.

The church was built at a cost of $24,000 and the work was done under the direction of Reverend Dominic Thomas O'Malley.

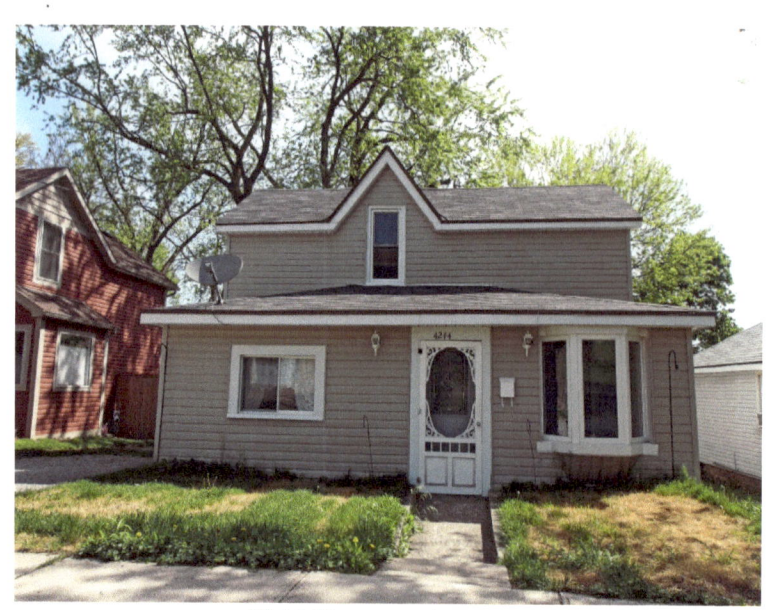

4244 Terrace Avenue

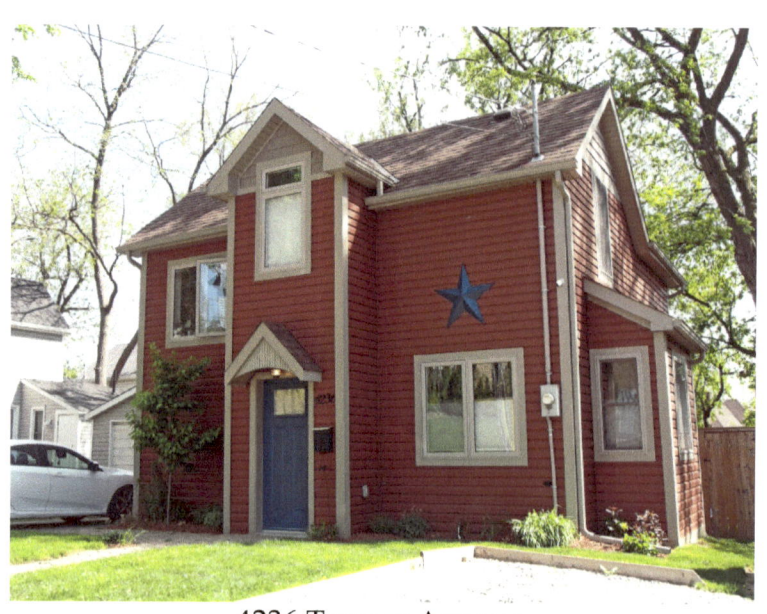

4236 Terrace Avenue

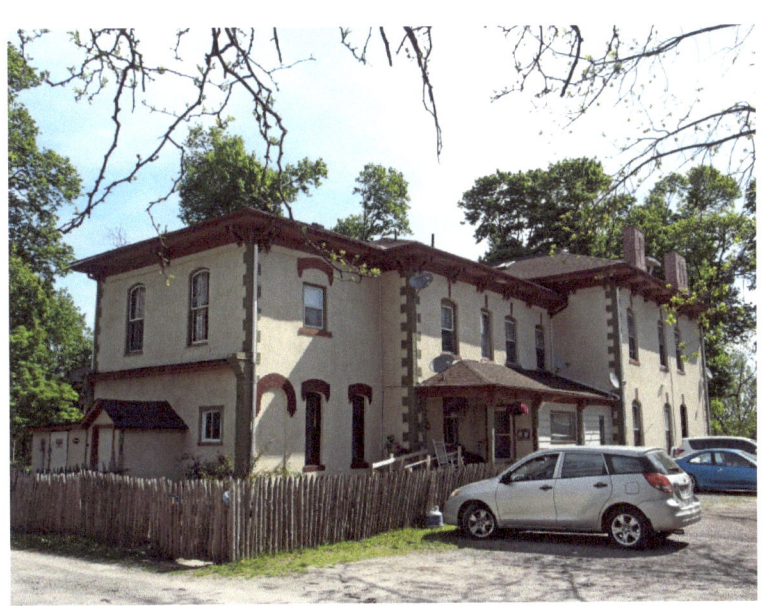

4223 Terrace Avenue - Glenview Mansion – 1870 - The house was built by John Drew on his 75 acre farm which he purchased in 1869. In 1881, he sold the house to Dr. John Ferguson who was twice elected Member of Parliament in 1882 and 1887. R. P. Slater, who served as mayor of Niagara Falls in 1899-1901, 1906-07, and 1909, purchased the house and lands in 1893.

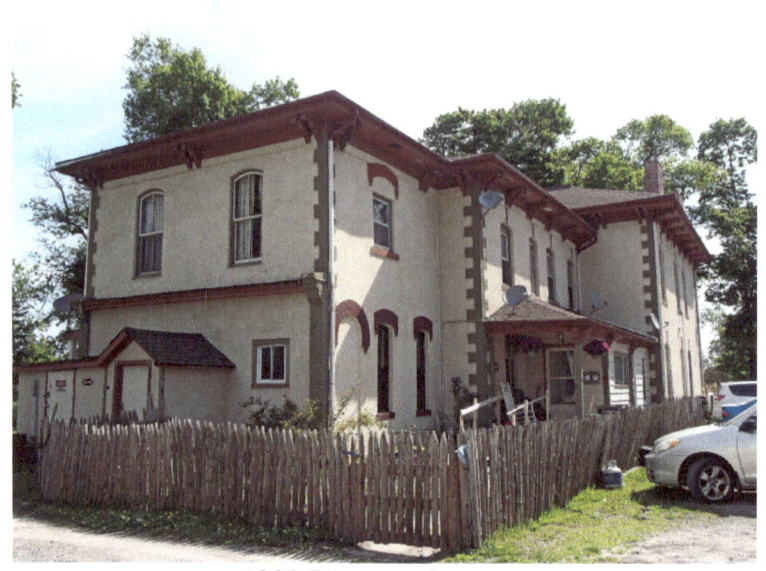

4223 Terrace Avenue

This large home has a square-plan main building and two rear wings. It was built in the Italianate style, and has a projecting central bay capped by a closed pediment and bay windows flanking the front entrance. Originally the roof had a belvedere surrounded by a wrought iron railing; it has been replaced by dormers. Brick was used to produce decorative elements such as quoins, window labels and the four large chimneys. Much of the brick has been covered with stucco.

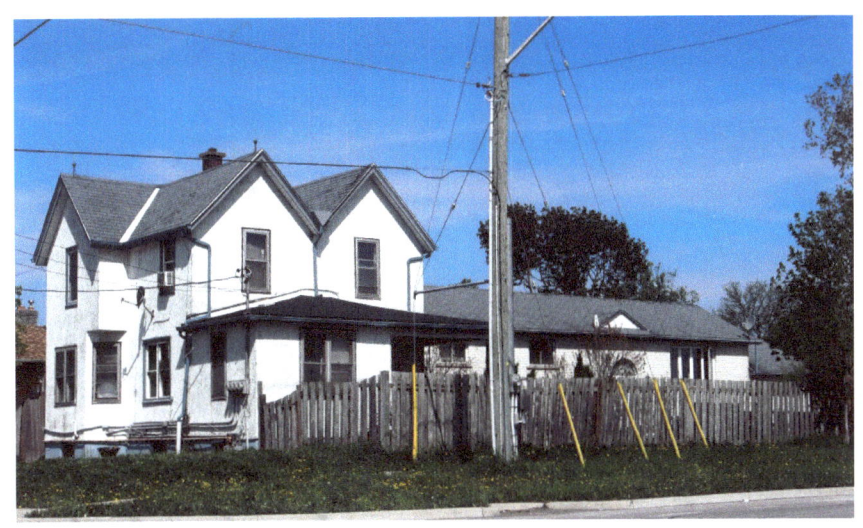

Church's Lane

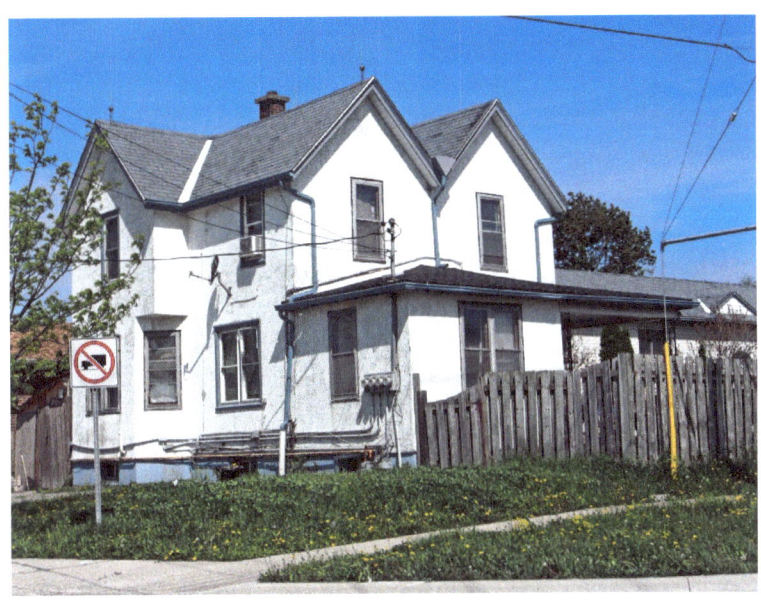

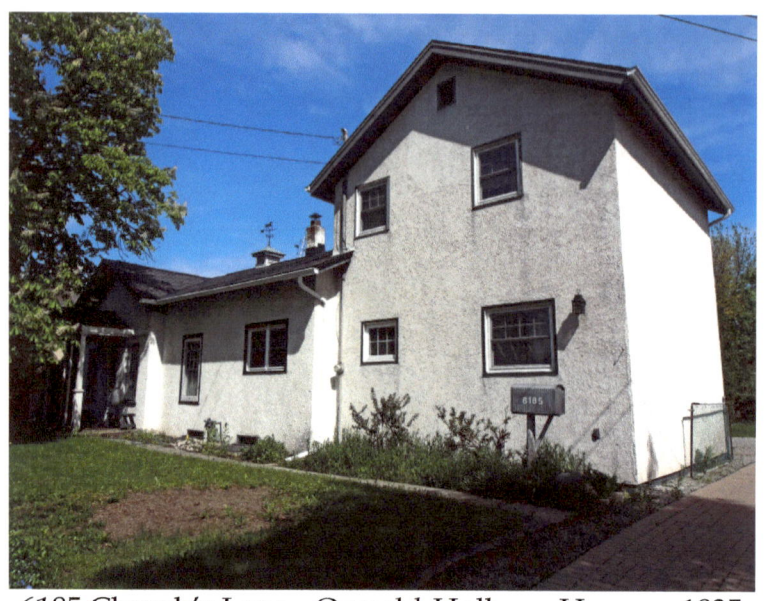

6185 Church's Lane - Oswald-Holburn House – 1835

    The west end of the present house was originally a two-room office building with brick walls of double thickness. This entire section is now the living room, with the original cast iron fireplace in the north end. The front porch is a recent addition. To the rear is a small brick smokehouse.
James Oswald, who lived in the house on the corner immediately to the west, used the office when managing his brewery which was located north of the railroad line on Highway 8.

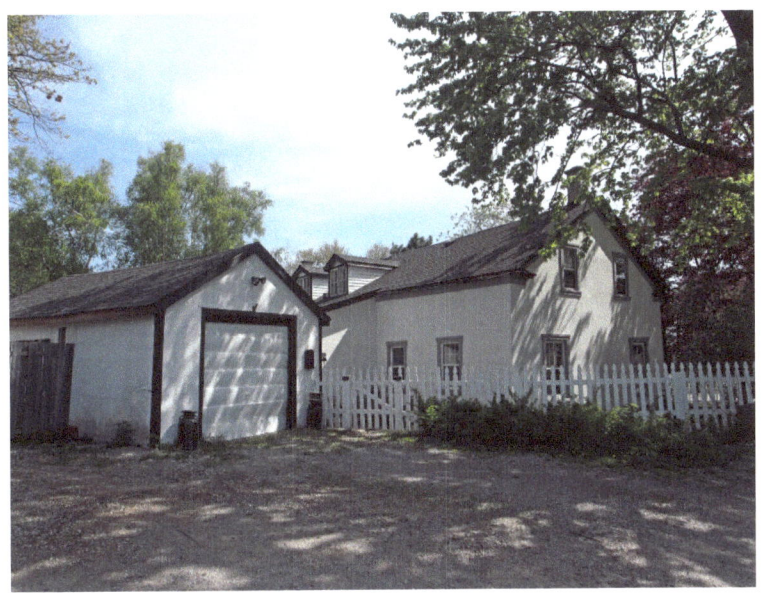

Church's Lane

Niagara Portage Road

Following the cession of the east bank of the Niagara River to the United States in 1783, the British authorities felt compelled to transfer the Portage Road around Niagara Falls to the west bank of the river. Opened in 1789 by a group of private traders led by Robert Hamilton, the road between Queenston and Chippewa became the official government route in 1791. Until the completion of the Welland Canal in 1829 and the building of railways in the 1850s, it was the main link in trade, travel, and war between Lake Ontario and the upper lakes.

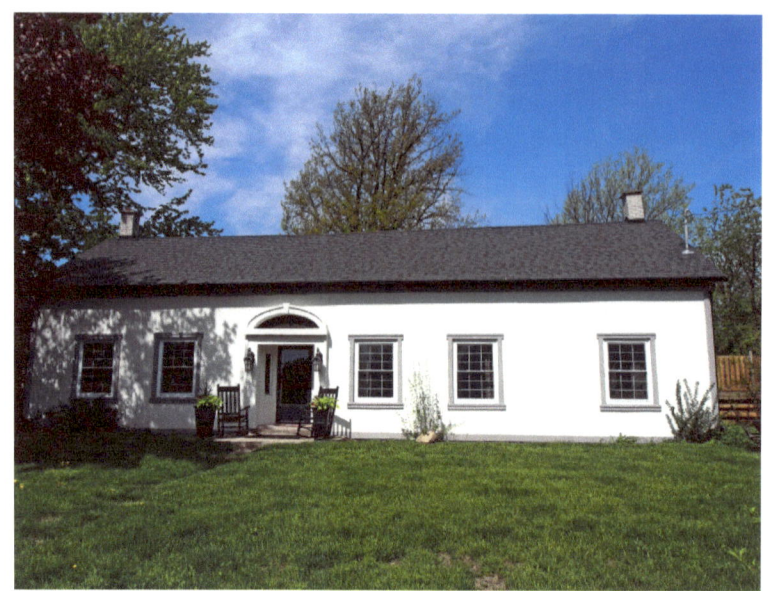

3011 Portage Road

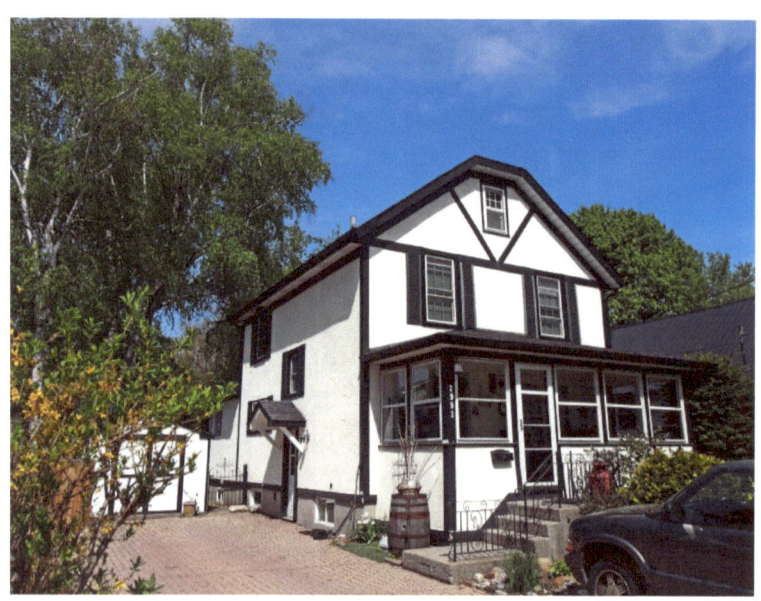

2993 Portage Road

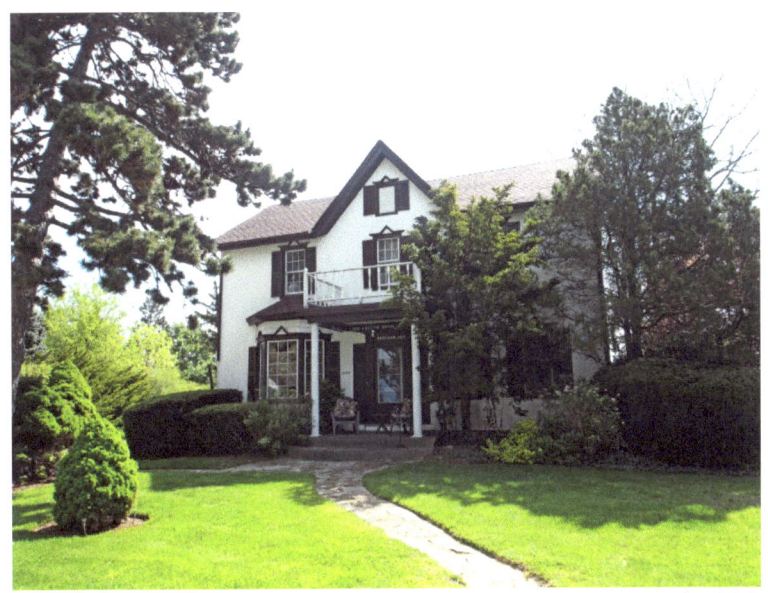

3000 Portage Road – The Church House - erected 1800

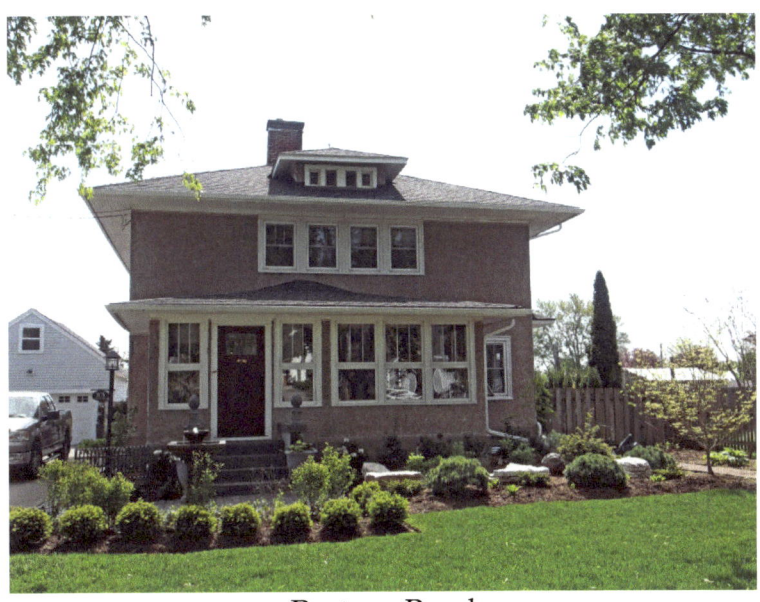

Portage Road

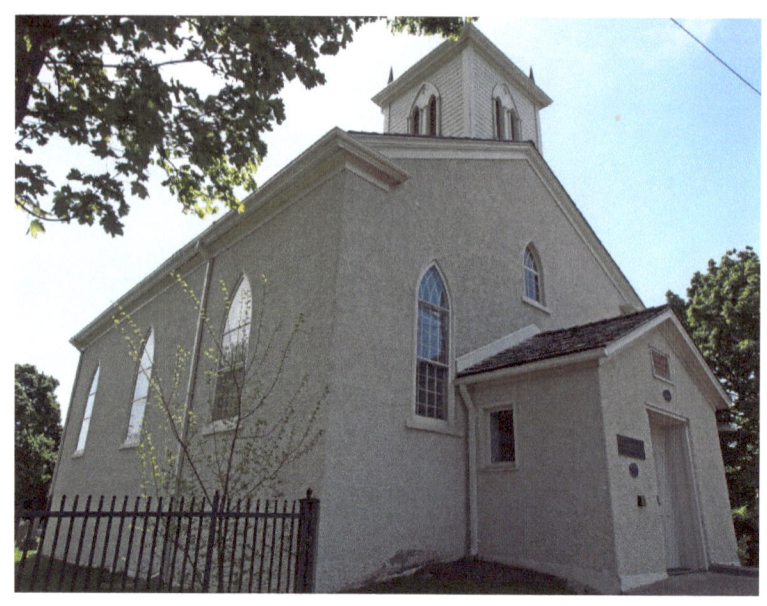

3394 Portage Road – Old Church of St. John the Evangelist – erected 1825 – simple rectangular structure, Gothic style lancet windows, square battlemented belfry

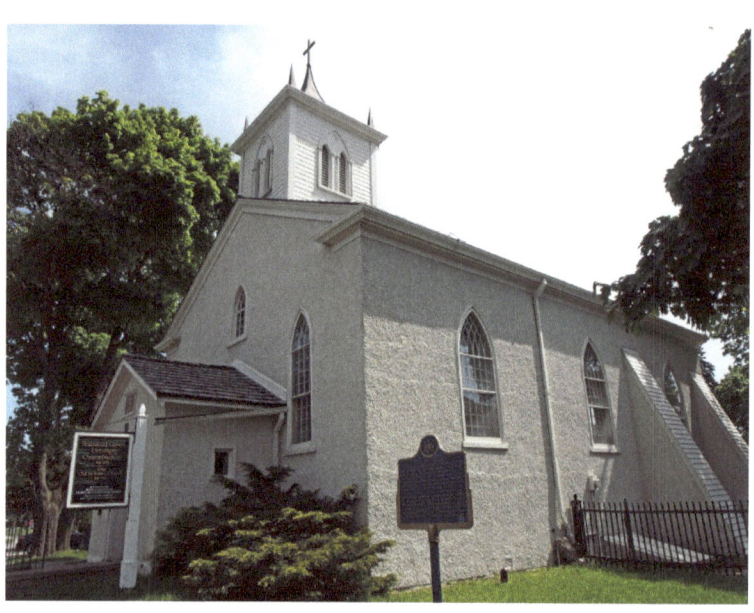

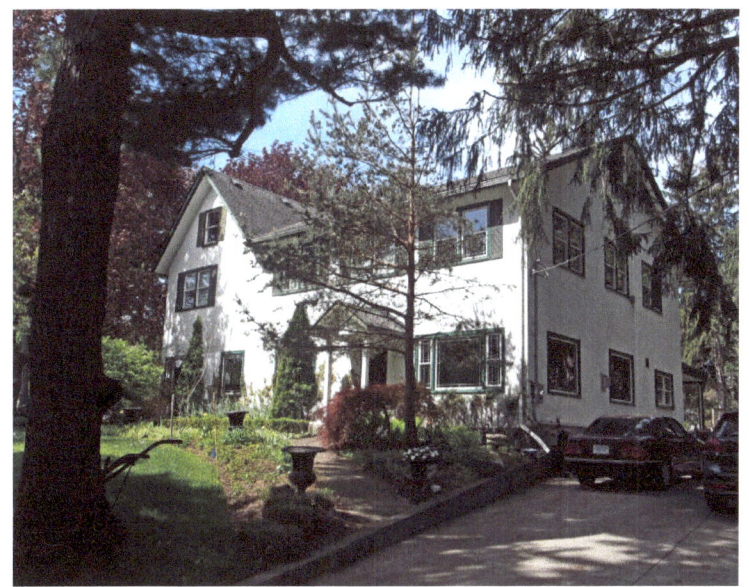

3227 Portage Road

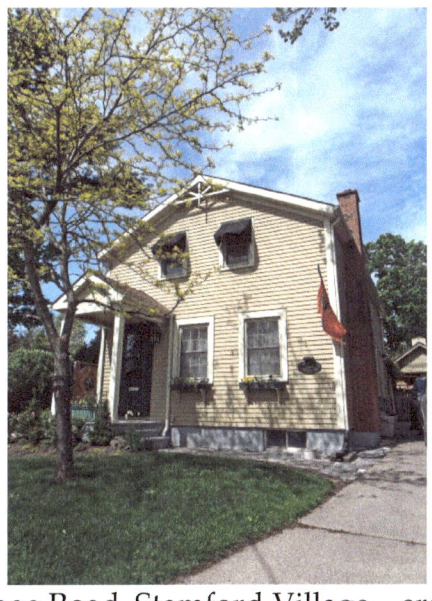

3165 Portage Road, Stamford Village – erected 1803

Stamford Green, Niagara Falls

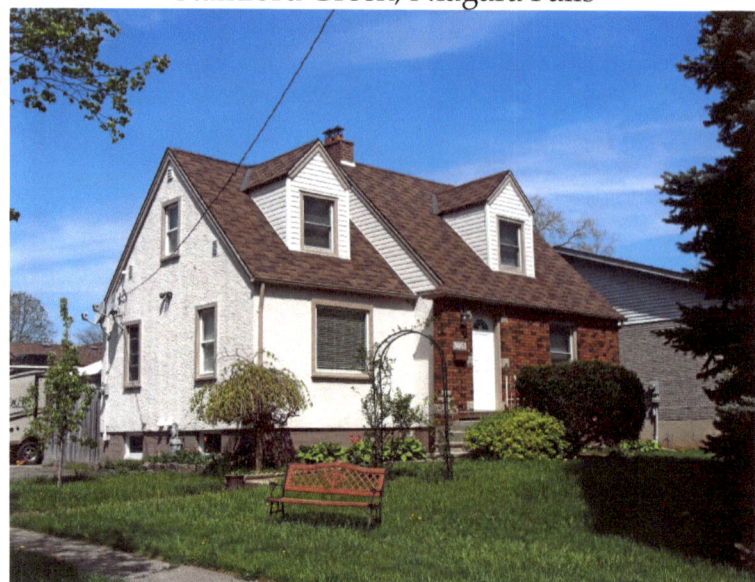

3053 St. Paul Avenue

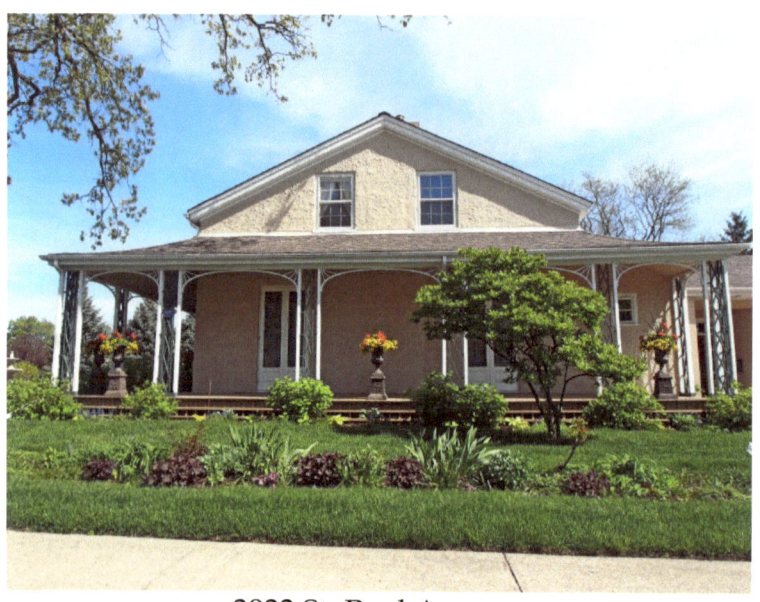

2922 St. Paul Avenue

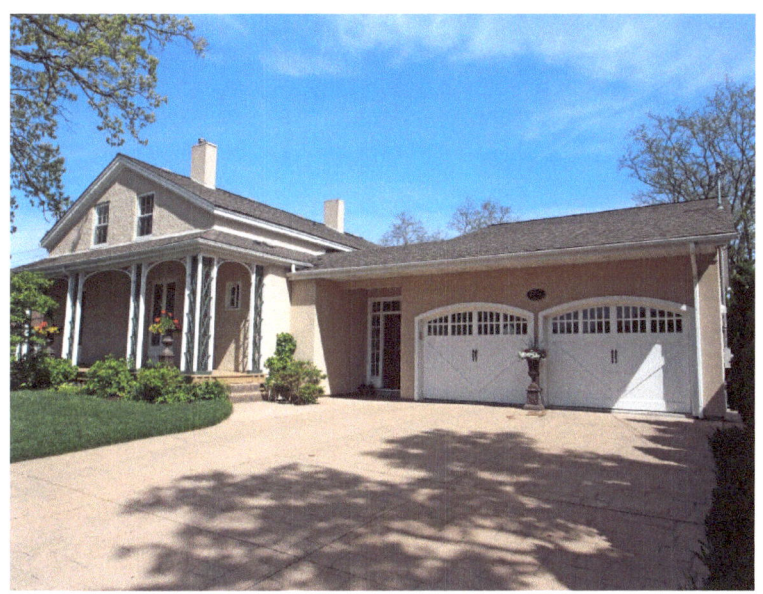

2922 St. Paul Avenue – Oswald House

James Oswald was a local businessman who owned a brewery with his brother near St. David's, co-founded the 1854 survey of Clifton with Samuel Zimmerman, and was proprietor of the Whirlpool Inn.

An excellent example of the Regency style, this house features large, multi-paned ground floor windows and a broad verandah with wood trellis supports across the south and west facades. The decorative iron fence, set in a stone base, along the south and west borders of the lot, was imported from England. It was built in 1835.

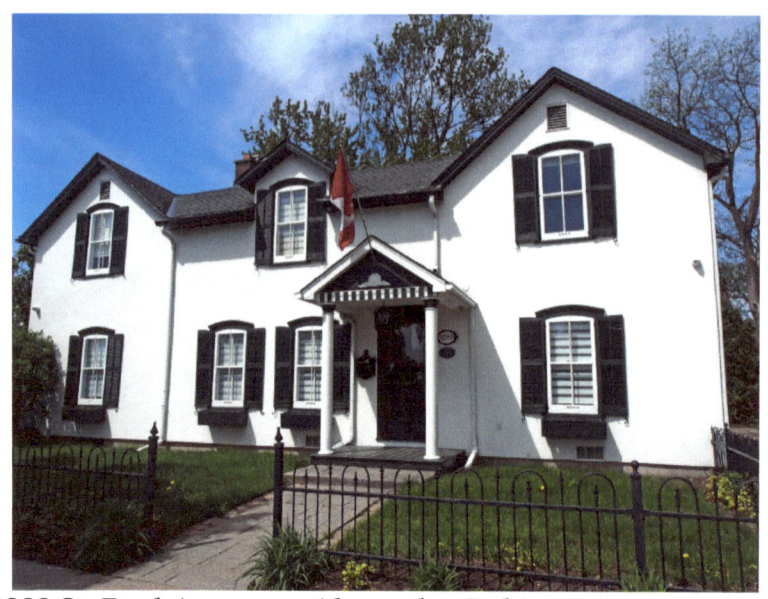

3289 St. Paul Avenue – Alexander-Robinson House - 1821

The house was owned by Susannah Alexander, widow of Hugh Alexander (1780-1817), the first merchant to open a store in Stamford. The original 2.5 acre lot later held a fruit farm, and the house offered accommodation for tourists beginning in the 1920s. The house was owned by the Robinson Family from 1913-1995.

The central part of the house was built earlier with squared timber walls lined with brick. The north and south gable ends were added later and the structure covered in clapboard and given its Italianate styling. In 1969, the interior was entirely renovated, the front porch was replaced and the exterior was covered in stucco.

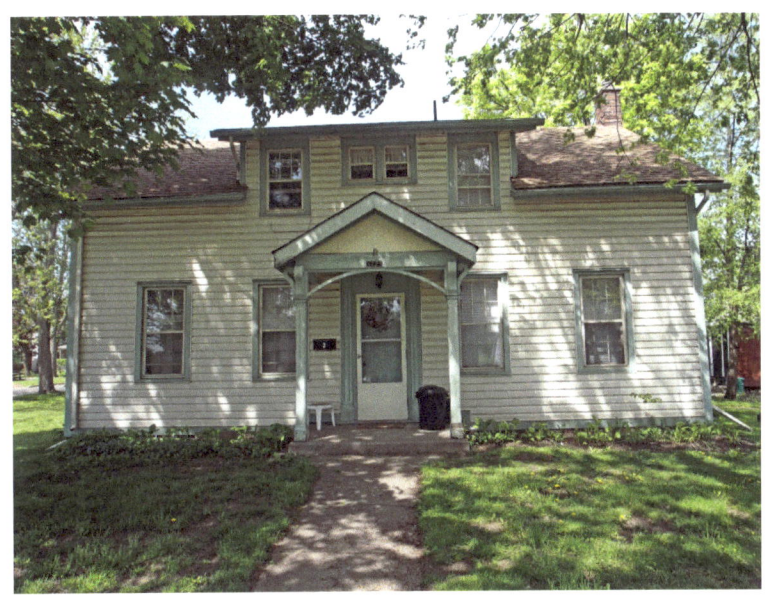

3221 St. Paul Avenue

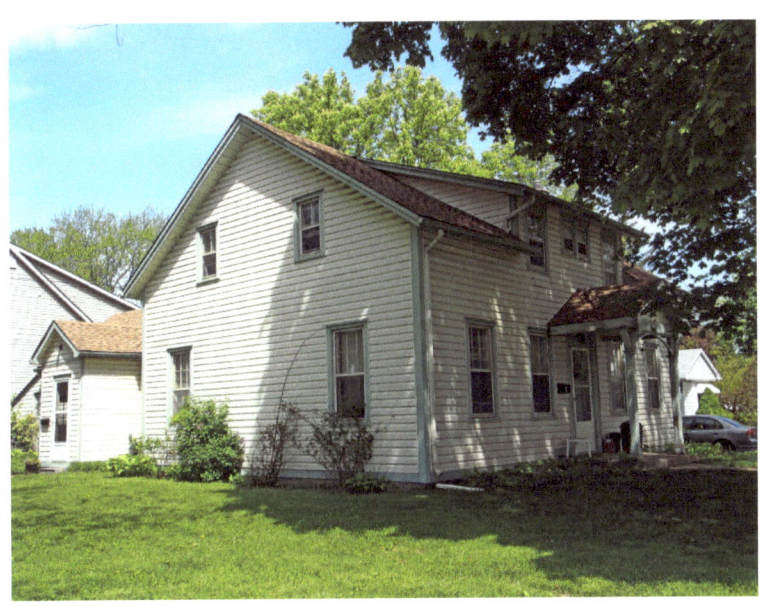

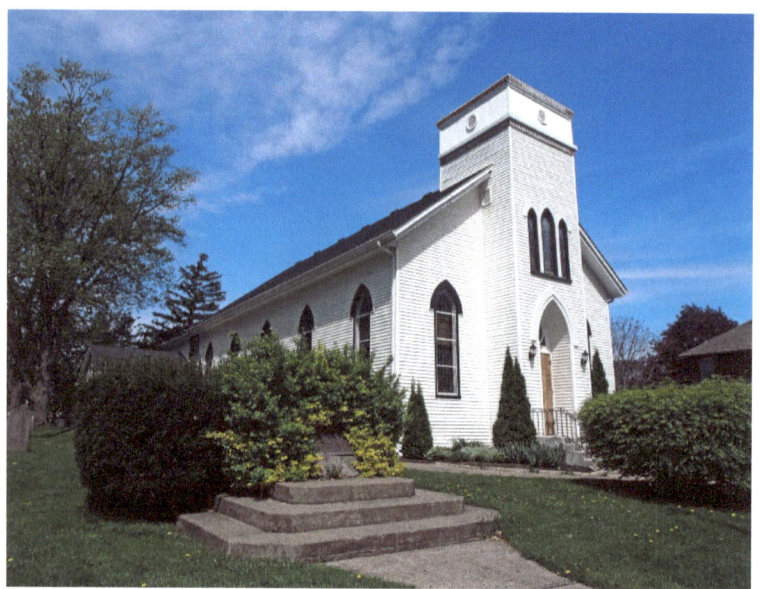

3121 St. Paul Avenue – Stamford Presbyterian Church - 1871

The original Presbyterian meeting house, built in 1791 of logs, served the earliest settlers of the area, many of whom were of Scottish descent who chose lands on top of the escarpment. The churchyard to the south, called "God's Half Acre" when it opened in 1784 is the resting place of many of Stamford's founding citizens.

The present church was built on the foundation of an earlier structure. Features of note are the balustrade on top and triple lancet windows on the front of the tower, and round stained glass window above the main door. The tower was originally three-sided with a back added later and each corner was once topped by a pinnacle.

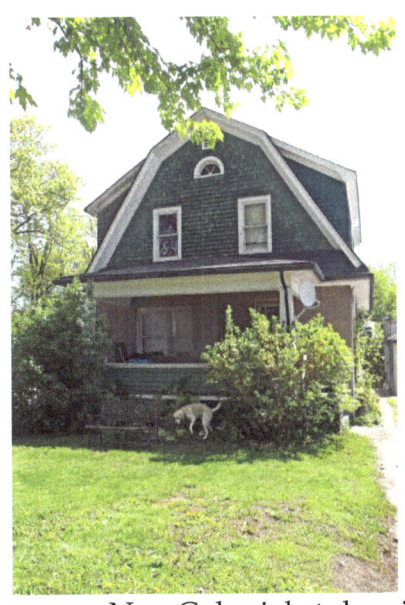

2728 St. Paul Avenue – Neo-Colonial style with gambrel roof

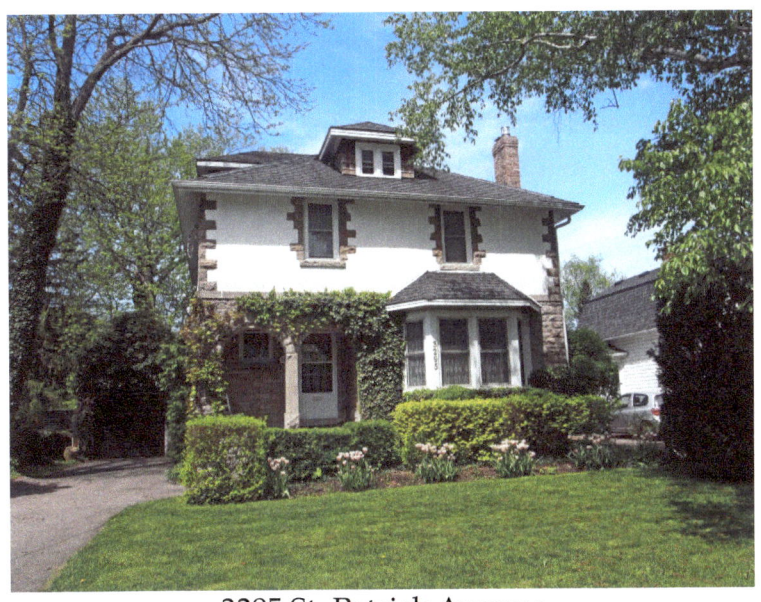

3295 St. Patrick Avenue

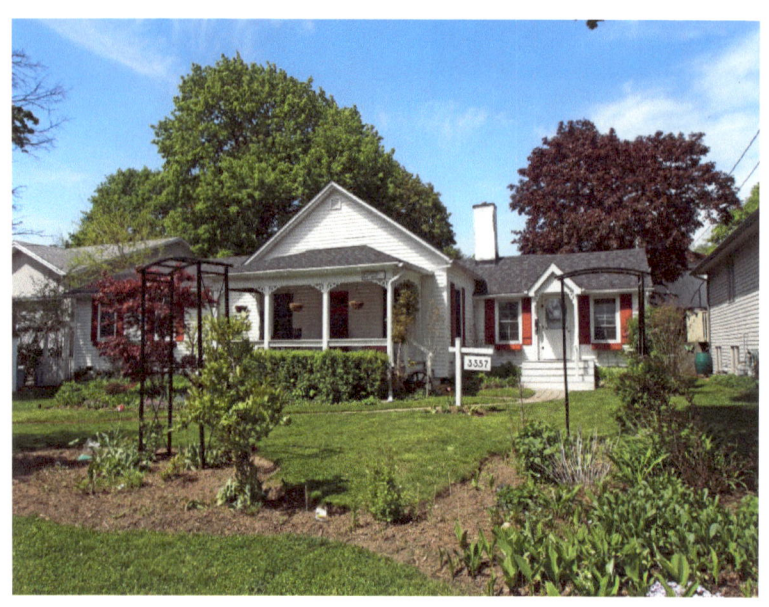

3357 St. Patrick Avenue – Toad Hall - 1805

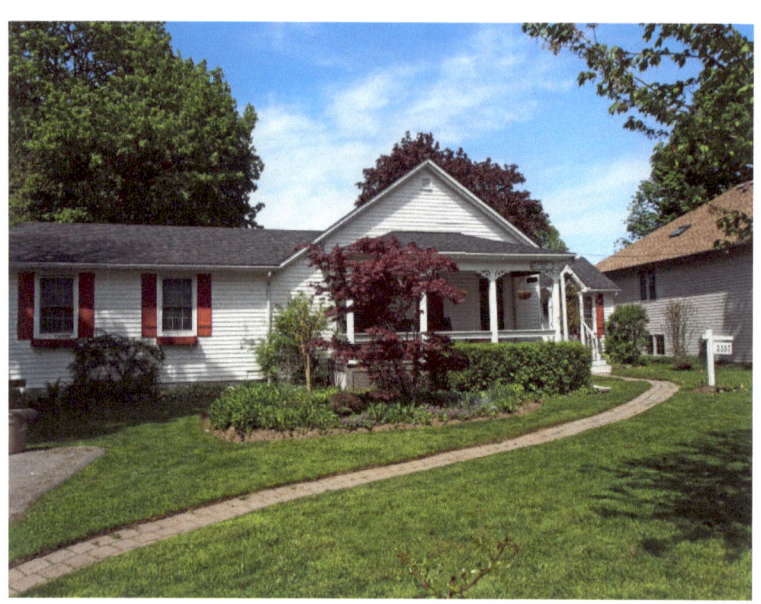

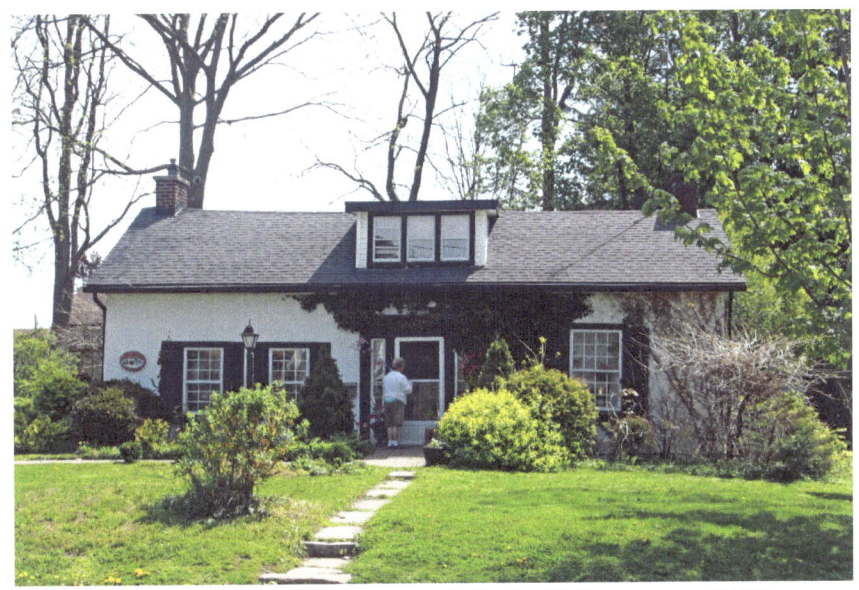

3360 St. Patrick Avenue - Mitchell Cottage - 1805

Also known as Stamford Cottage, the original cabin was built on Crown Land granted to the Presbyterian Church to assist early settlers. It was later owned by John Hawkins from 1837 to 1853, and it is to him that the 1840s appearance of the house is attributed.

The house was constructed as a log cabin (smaller than the present structure) with heavy timber beams and a stone foundation. In the 1840s, an extension was built on the south end, and Classical Revival elements such as eave returns and a "Georgian Wilderness" type door were added. The exterior is covered with stucco.

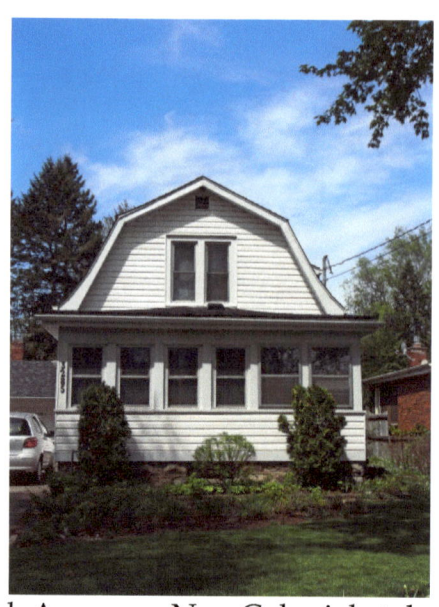

3285 St. Patrick Avenue – Neo-Colonial style, gambrel roof

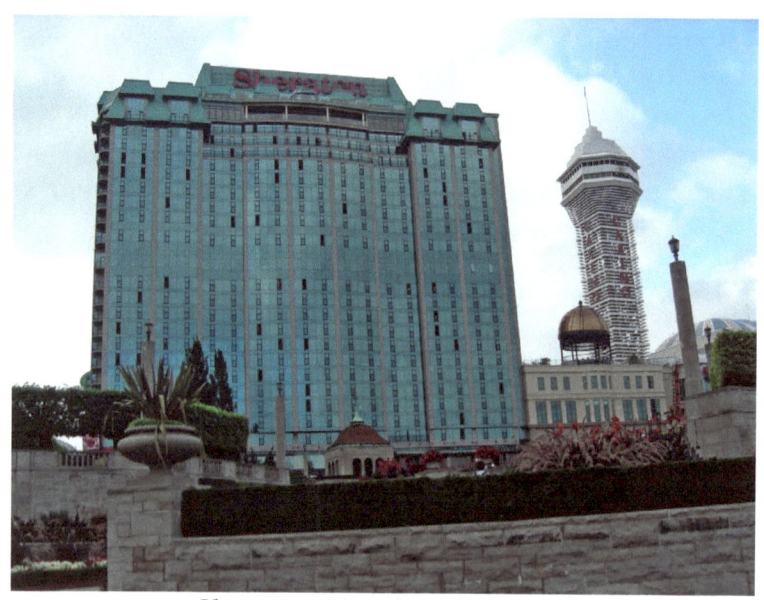

Sheraton Hotel and Casino

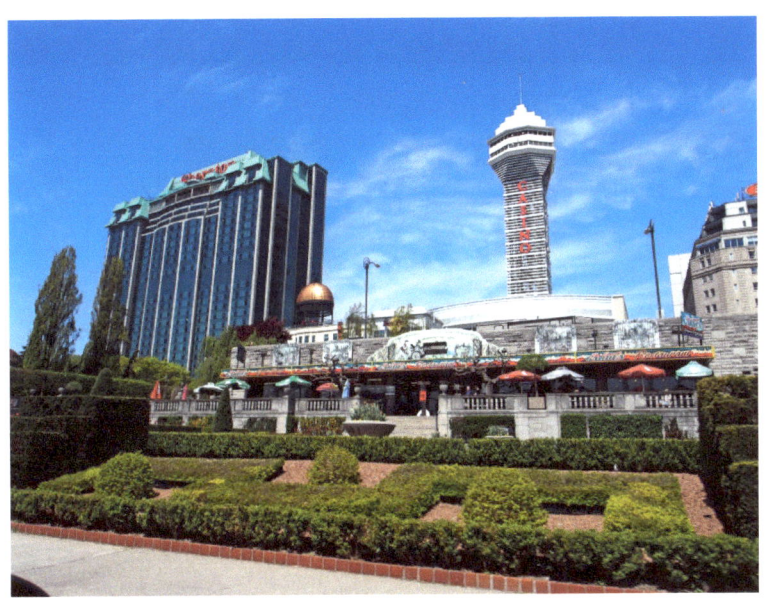

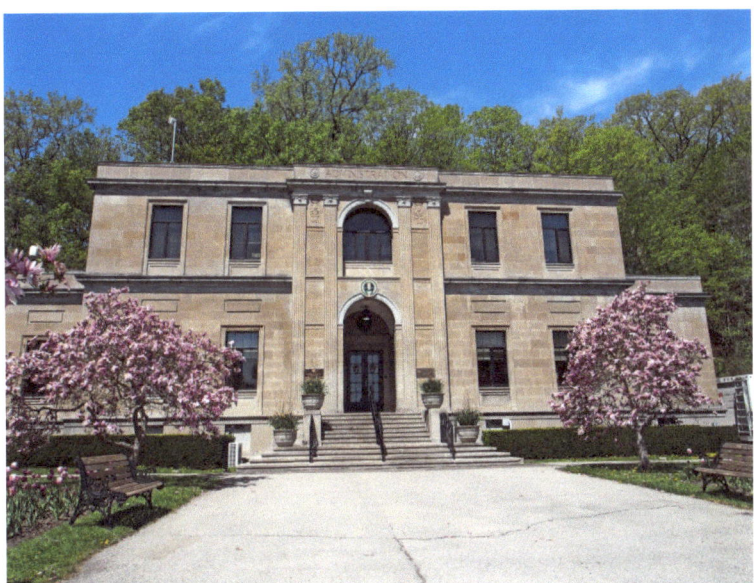

The Niagara Parks Commission Police Department

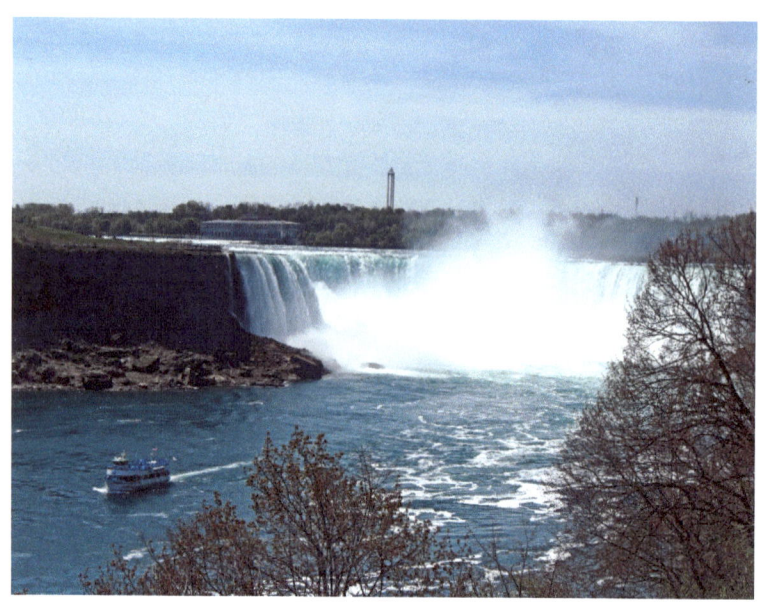

Horseshoe Falls

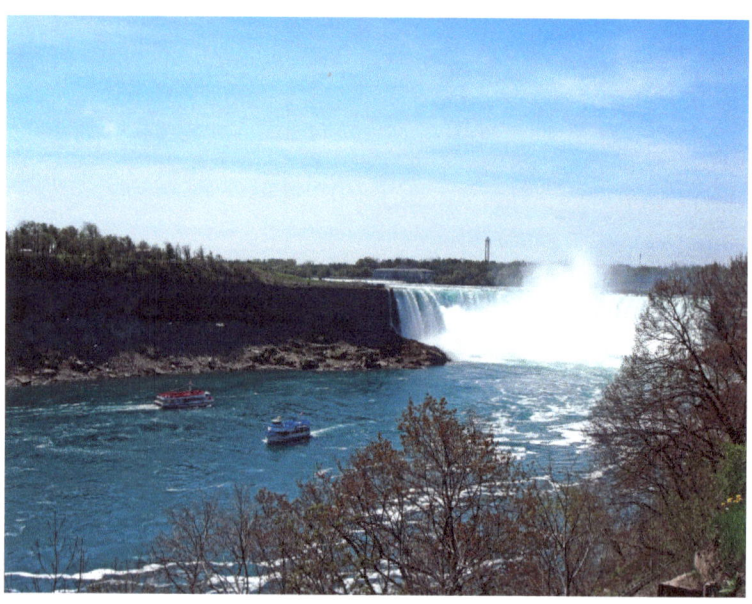

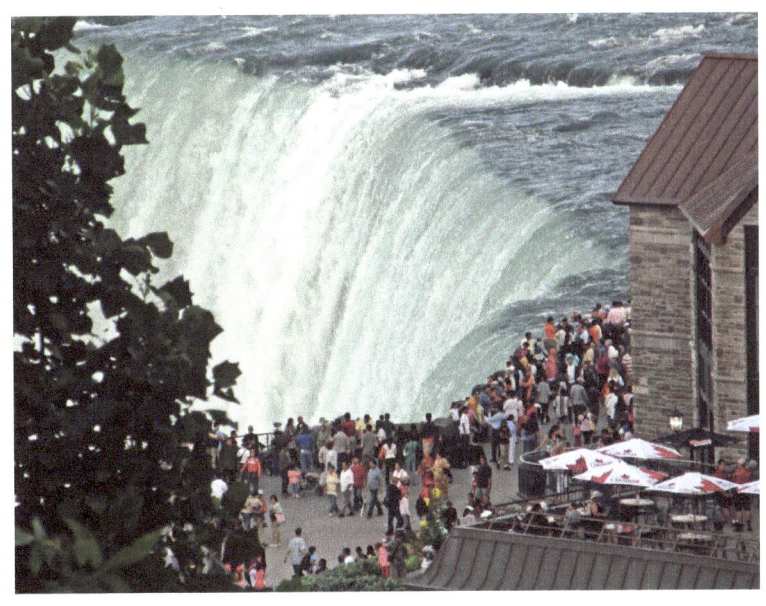

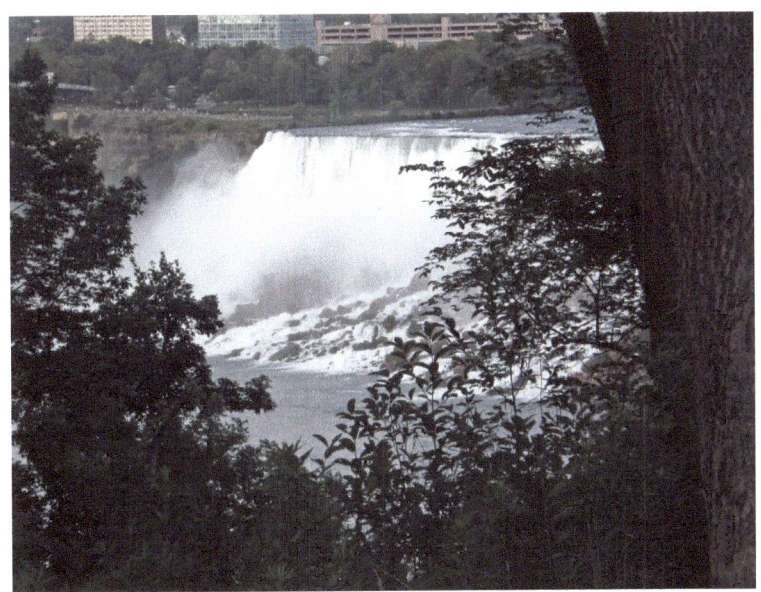

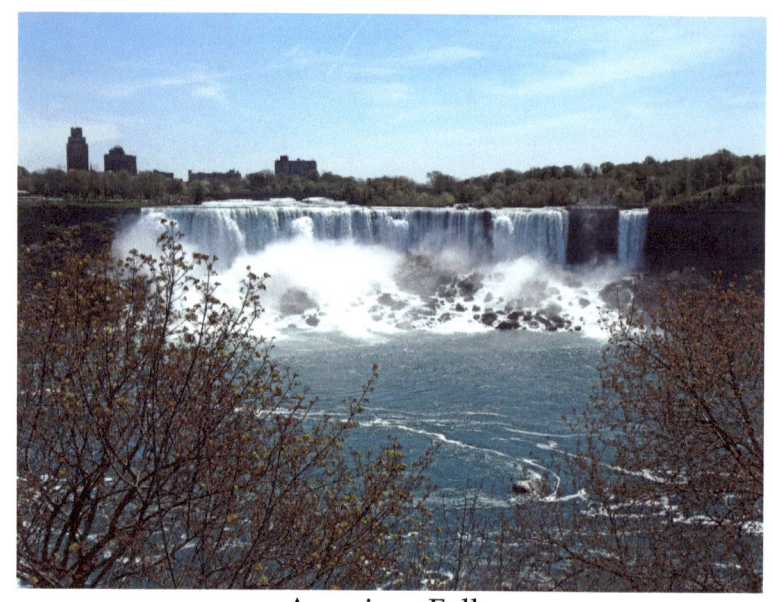

American Falls

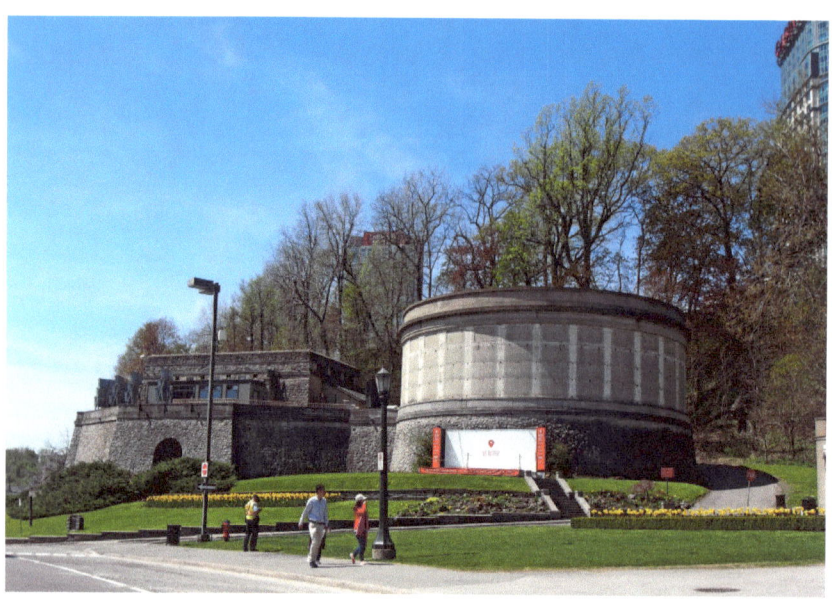

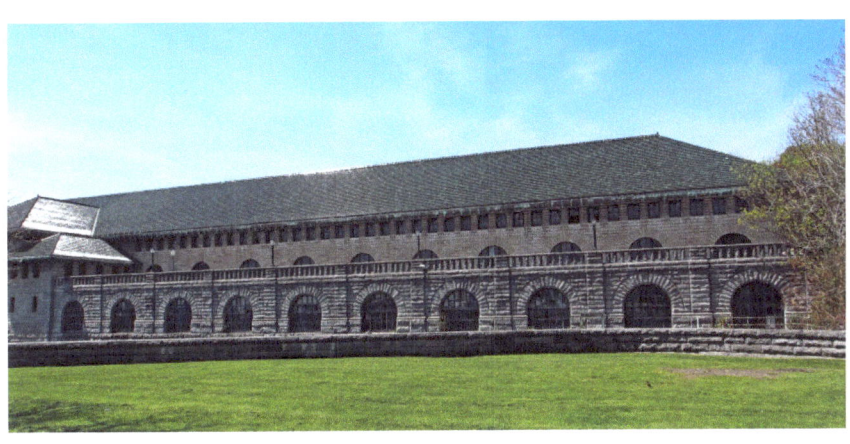

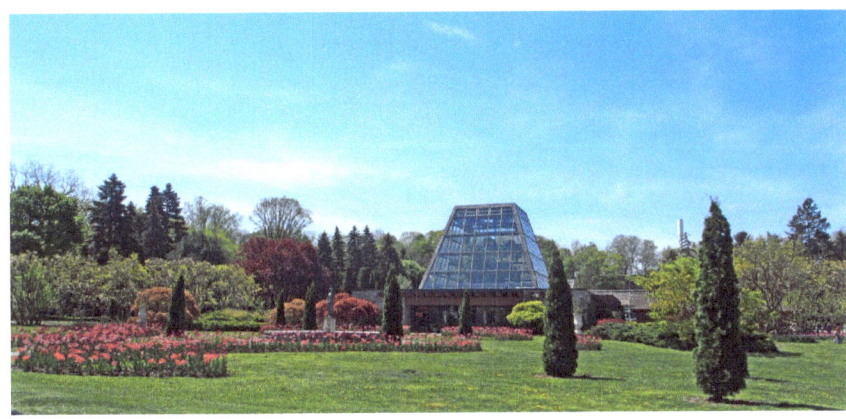

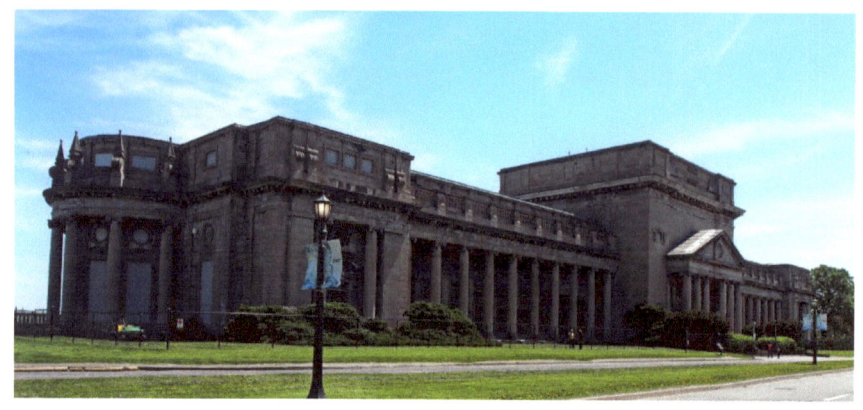

Electrical Development Company of Ontario Limited – 1906

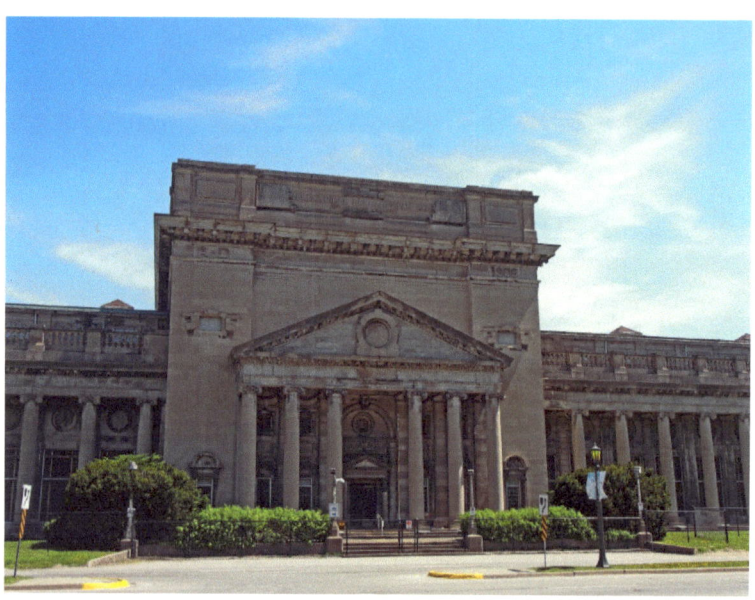

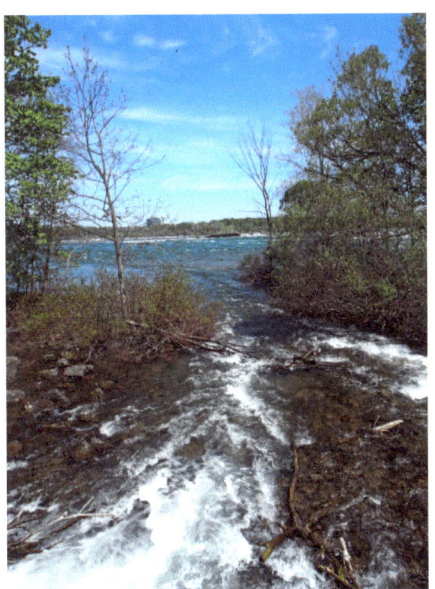

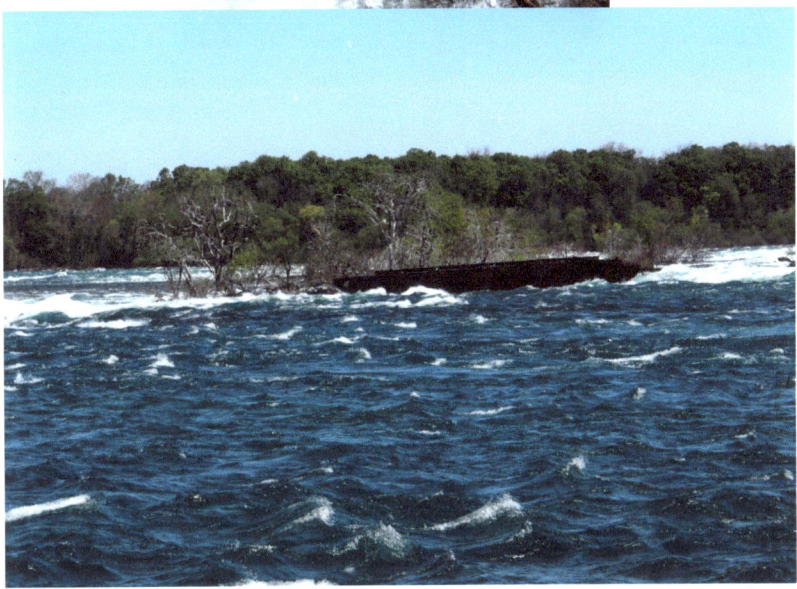

Stranded Skow – on August 6, 1918 this dumping scow broke loose from its towing tug about 1.6 kilometers (1 mile) upriver with two men on board. They opened the bottom dumping doors and the scow grounded in the shallow rapids. The men were rescued the next day.

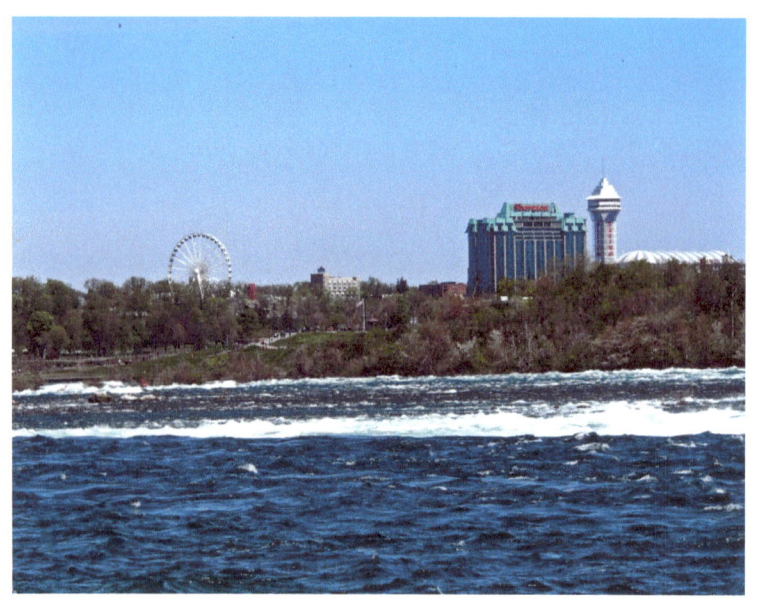

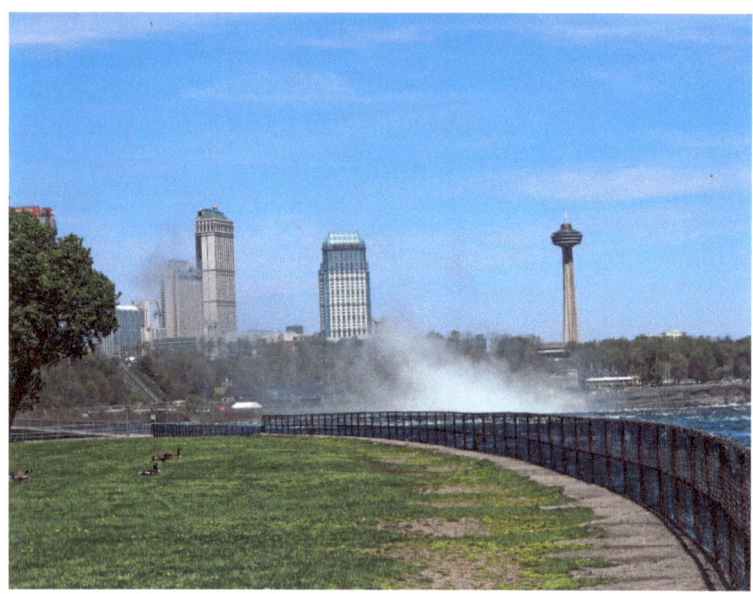

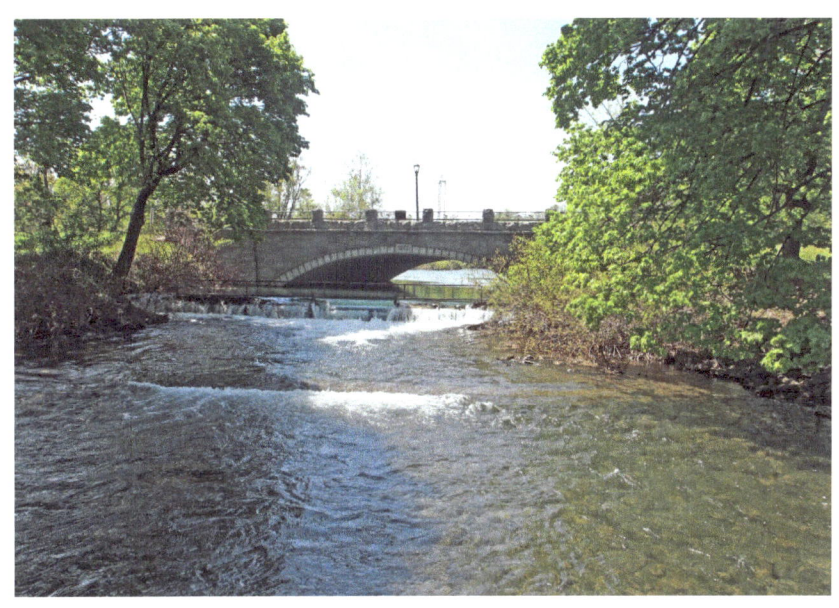

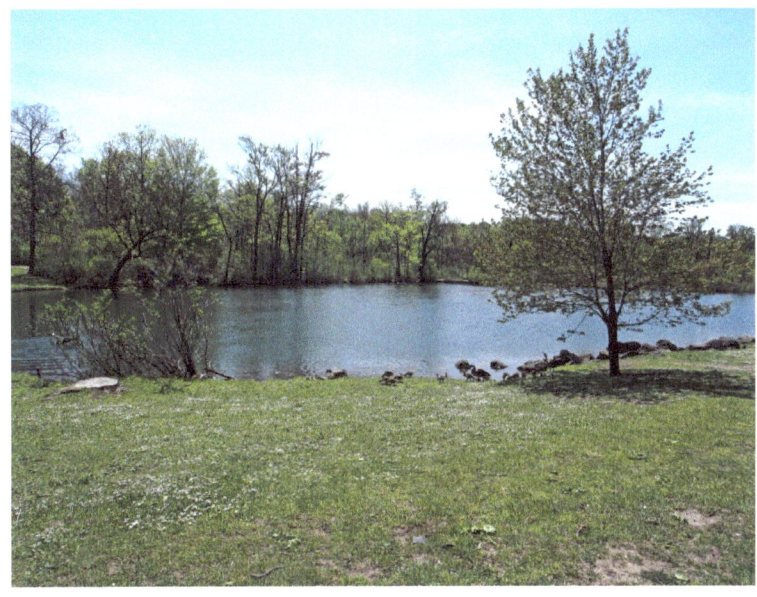

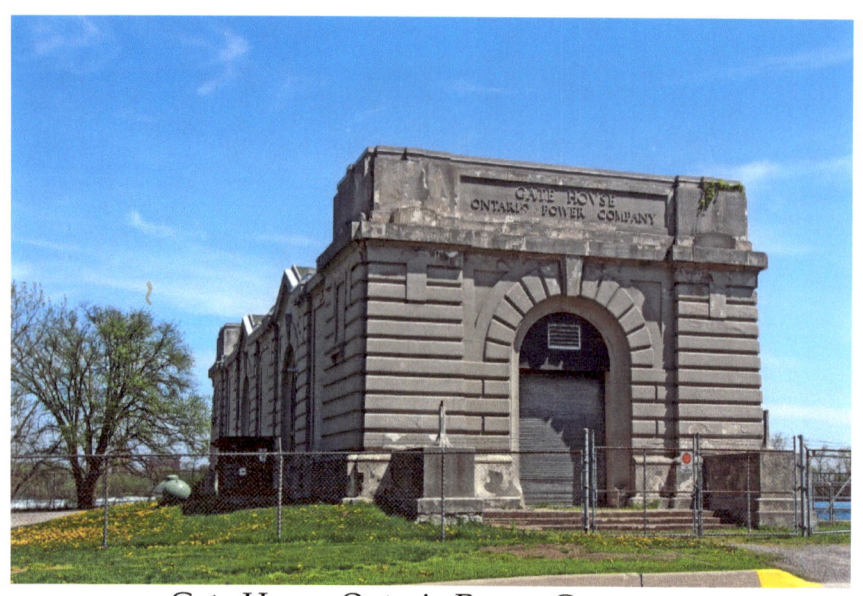

Gate House Ontario Power Company

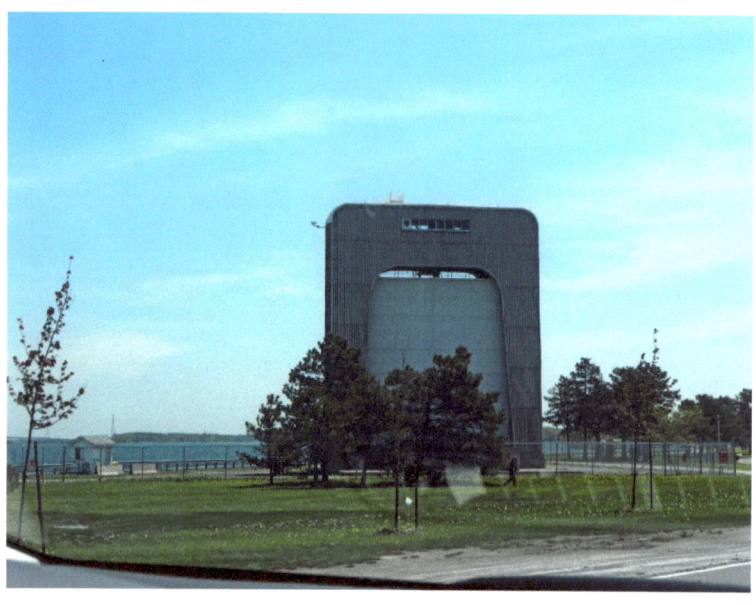

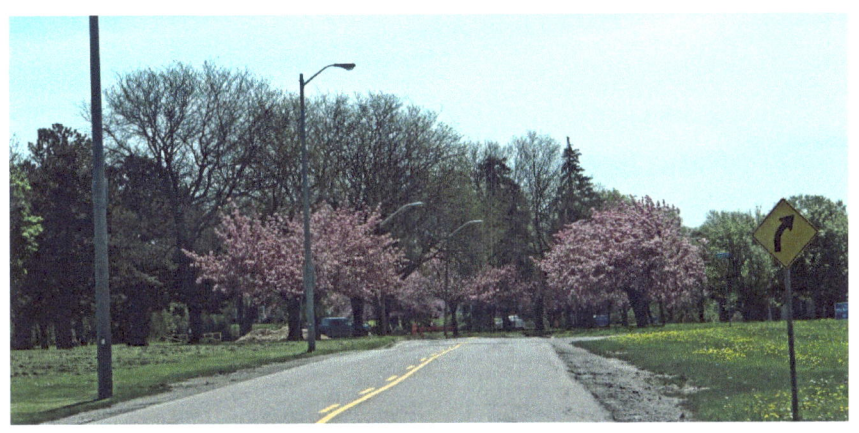

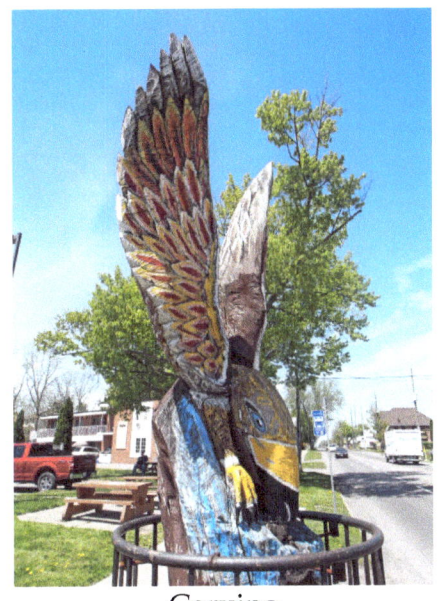
Carving

Chippawa

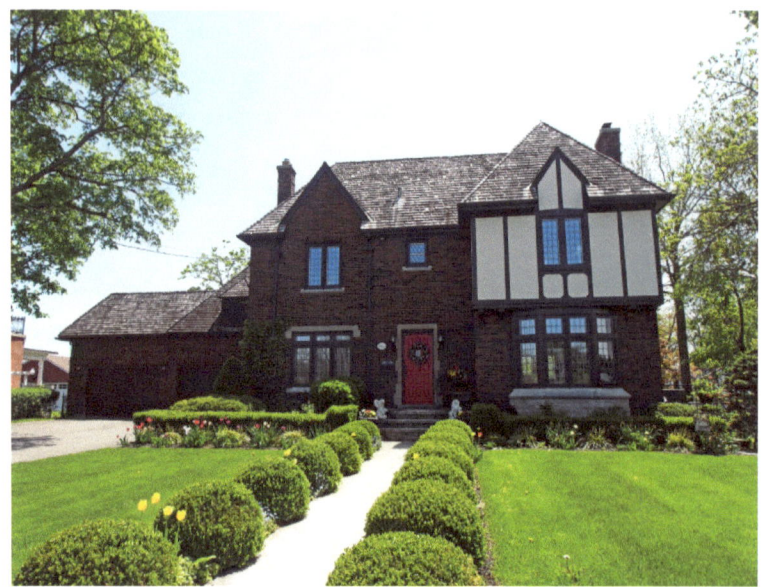

3634 Bridgewater Street

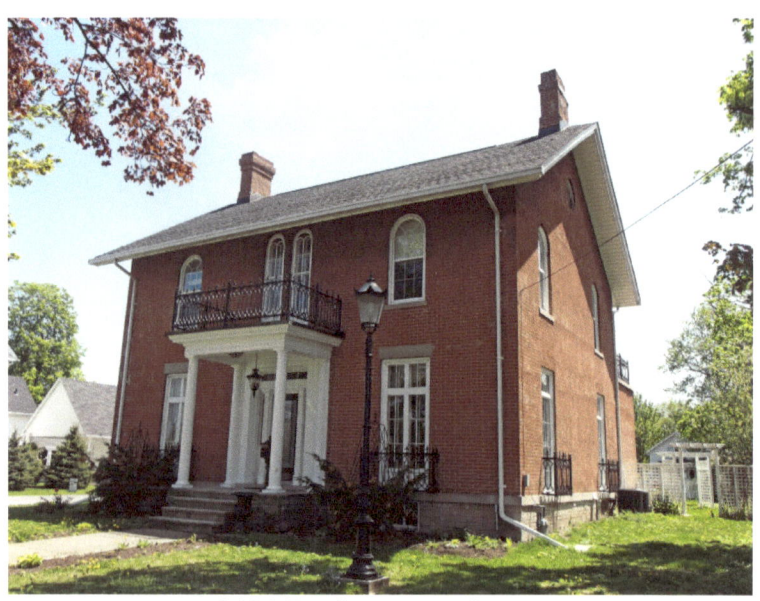

3624 Bridgewater Street

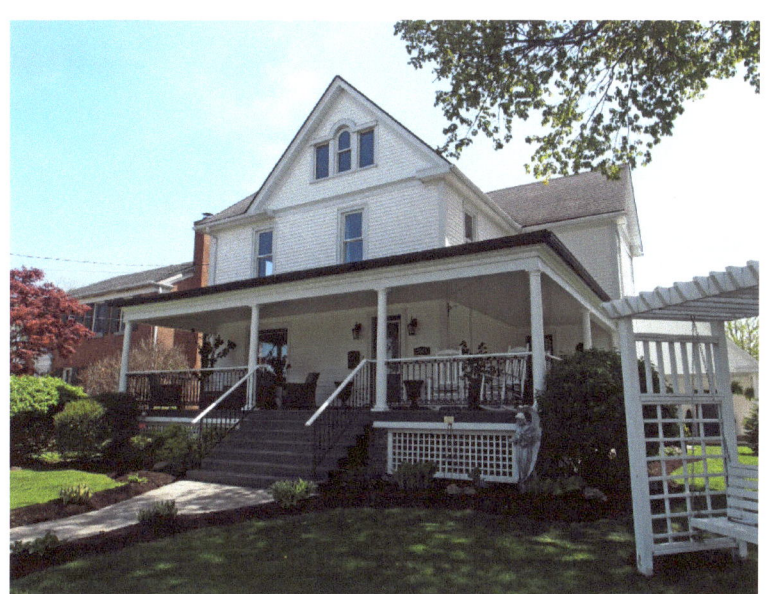
3604 Bridgewater Street

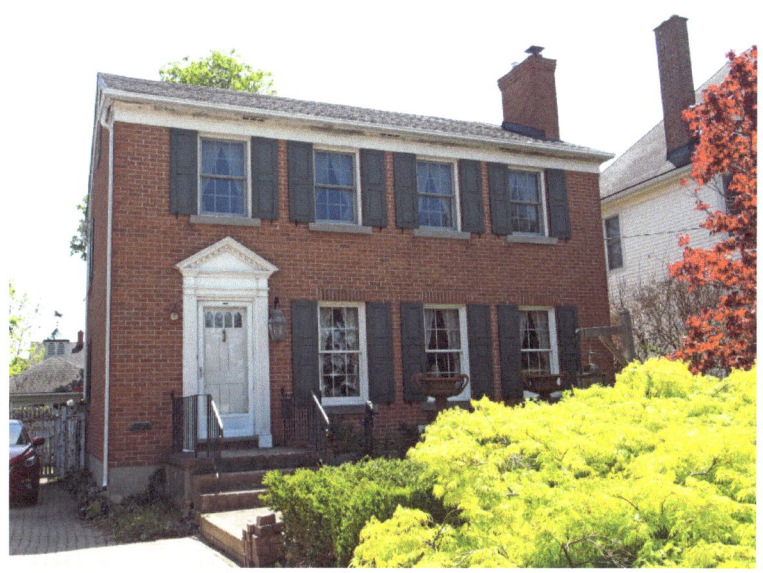
3594 Bridgewater Street

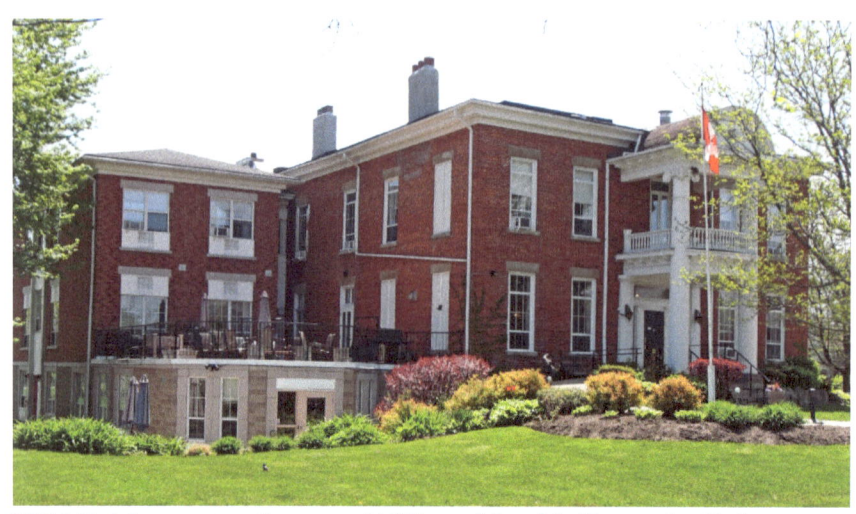

3584 Bridgewater Street – Willoughby Hall was built between 1830 and 1840 by James Cummings, one of the incorporators of the Erie and Ontario Railroad, the first railway in Upper Canada.

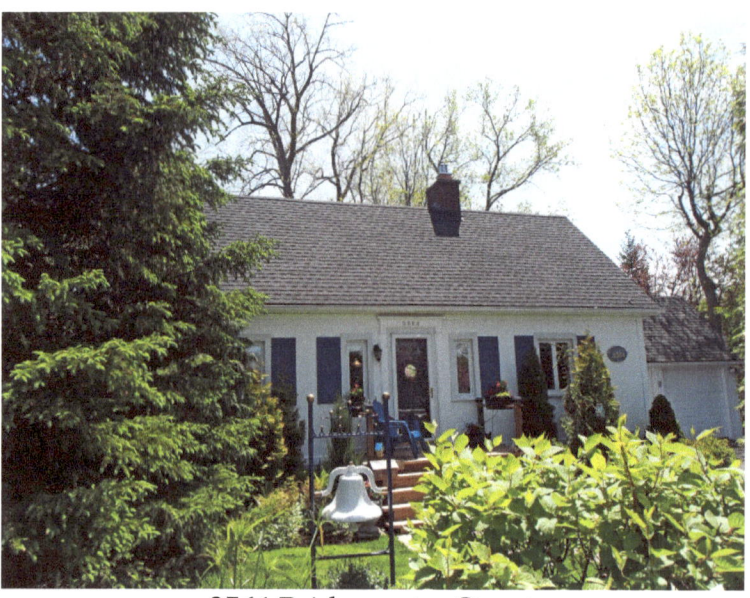

3564 Bridgewater Street

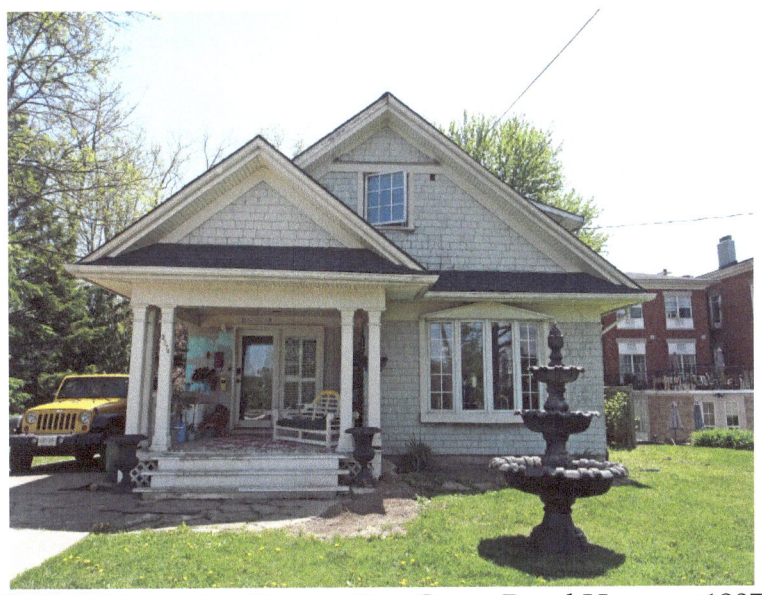

3574 Bridgewater Street - Ray Corry Bond House – 1907

    This was the home of Ray Corry Laura Bond, who was an active community worker and supporter. She did extensive research into Chippawa's past that resulted in a book entitled *Peninsula Village*. Mrs. Bond was born in Stamford Township in 1885 and graduated from Trinity College and the Ontario Teacher's College. She married James R. Bond in 1914. The couple lived in this house, the Riverview Cottage, which had been Ray's home since 1907. Mrs. Bond was honored with a Canada Centennial Medal in 1967. She lived in this cottage until her death in 1970.

    This is a vernacular style shingled cottage.

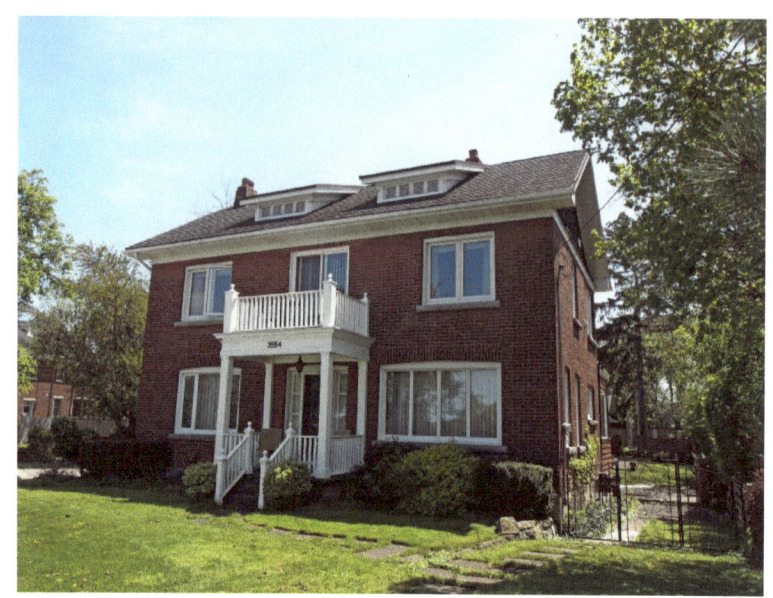

3554 Bridgewater Street

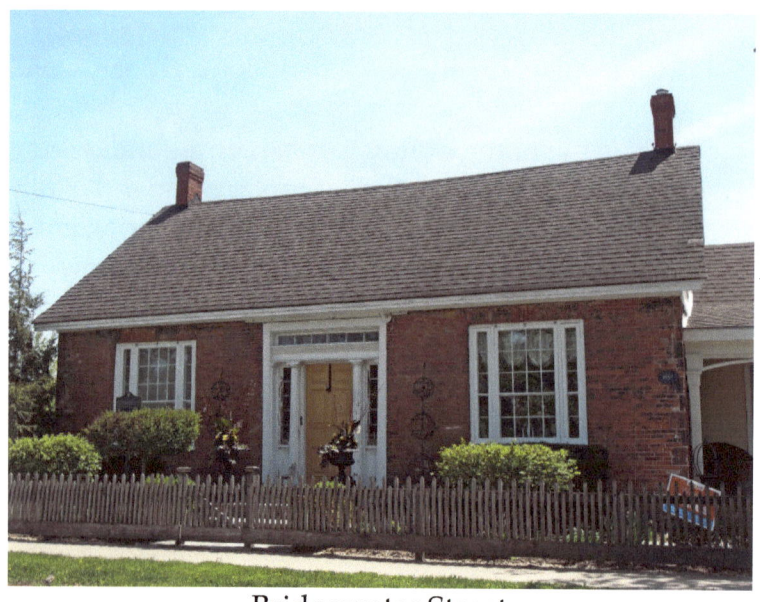

Bridgewater Street

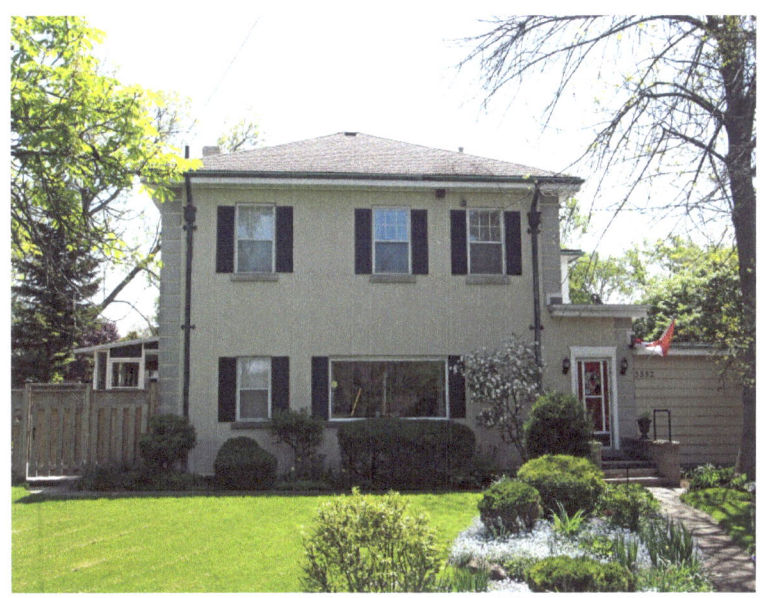

3552 Bridgewater Street - Mcglashan/Thomas House - 1854

The Mcglashan/Thomas house has been the residence of several individuals responsible for the economic growth of Chippawa and of the Niagara area. Built during Chippawa's golden age as a port and manufacturing center in the 1850s, it was for a short time the home of James Mcglashan, a local merchant and later longtime treasurer of Welland County. John Thomas and his family were involved in the establishment of local industry, co-founder of a major distillery and a grist mill. In the 20th century, C. Ellison Kaumeyer as Director of Niagara Parks & Bridge Commission worked towards the restoration of Niagara's past as well as the development of its transportation network.

The earliest part of the house, closest to Main Street, was two stories and square in plan. The two-story house is now rectangular in plan. It is of wood frame construction with a red brick veneer which is now covered with stucco. The façade is arranged around three regularly spaced bays. The style of the house is derived from principles of balance and proportion associated with Neo-Classical traditions.

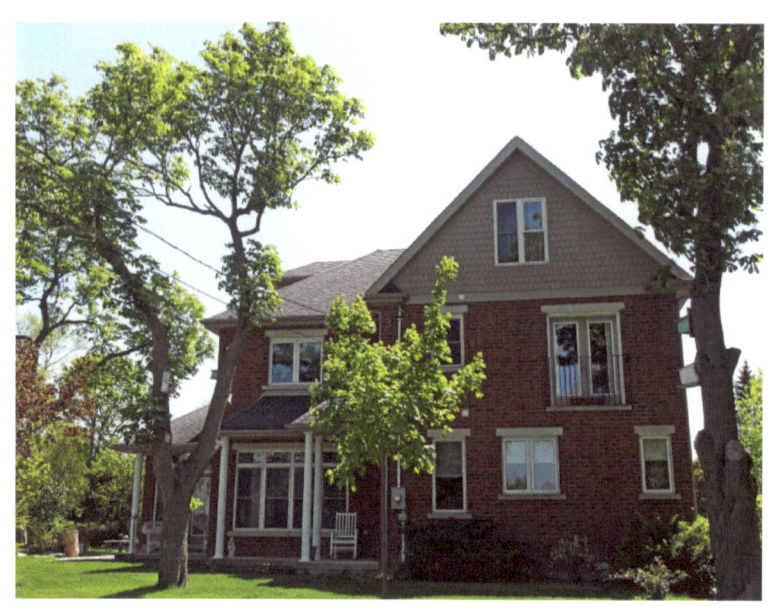

Bridgewater Street

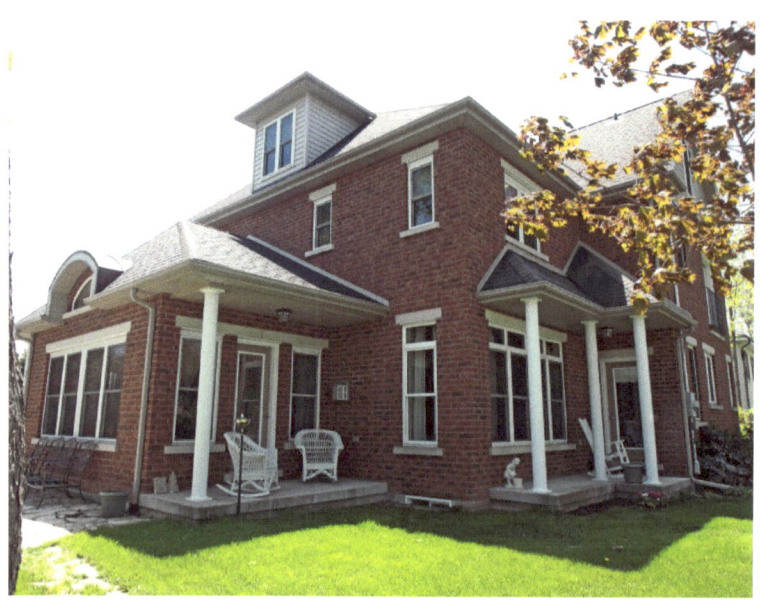

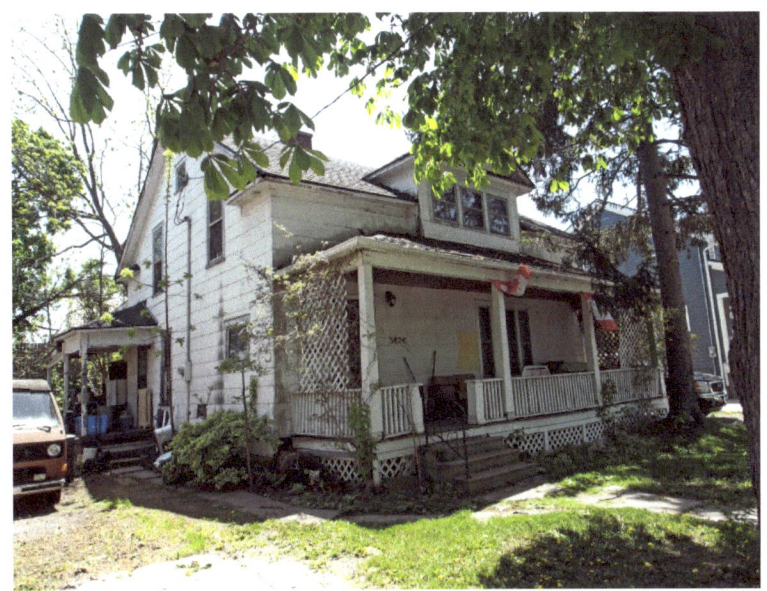

3824 Bridgewater Street

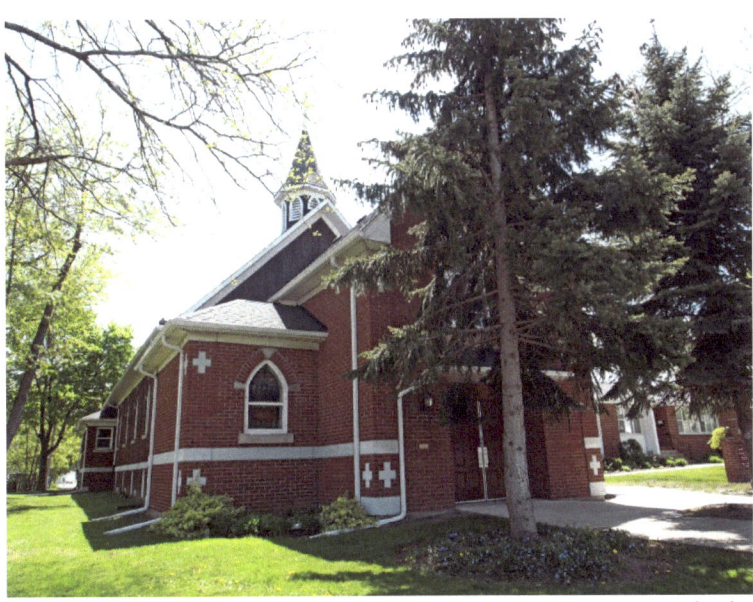

3882 Main Street - Sacred Heart Parish Roman Catholic Church

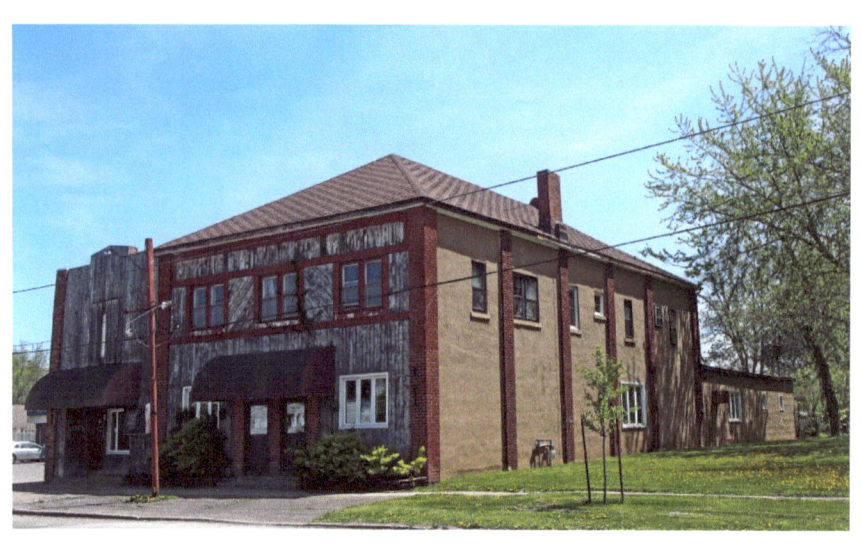

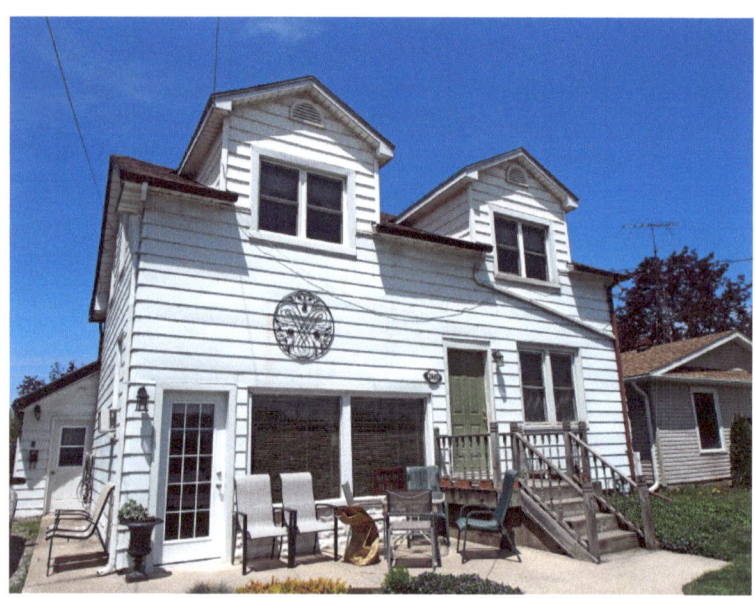

3865 Main Street

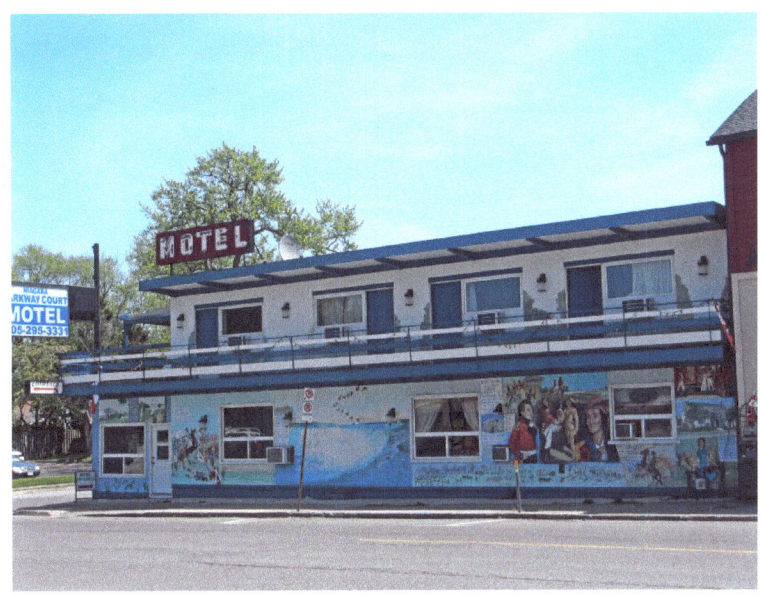

3708 Main Street West – Niagara Parkway Court Motel

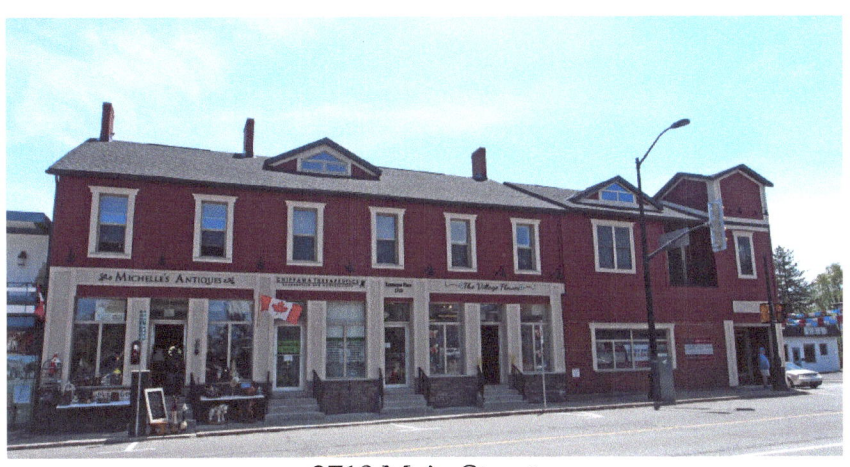

3710 Main Street

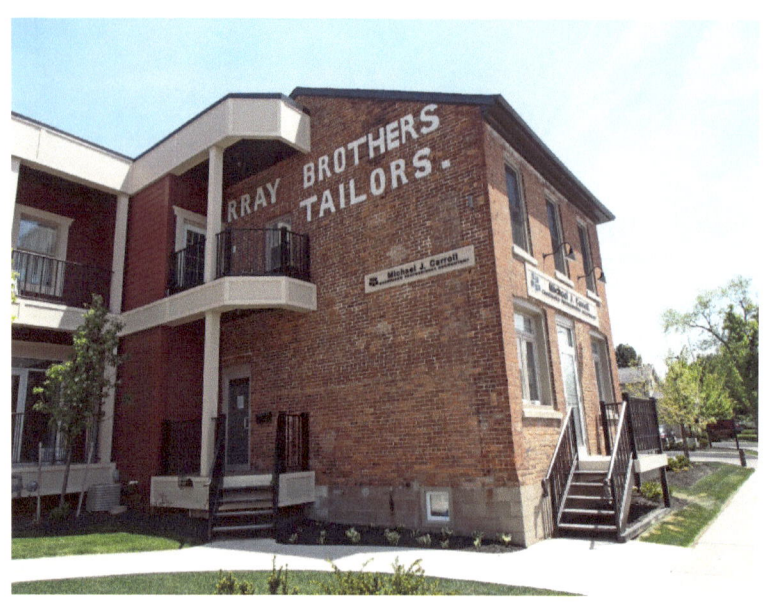

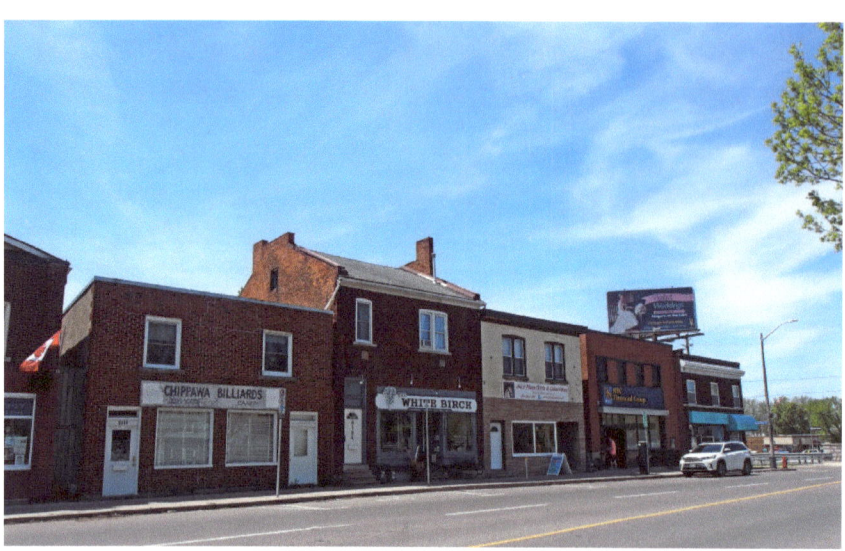

8178-8188 Cummington Square West

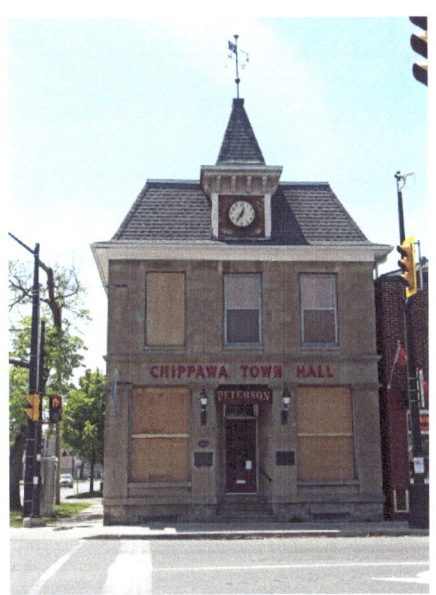

8196 Cummington Square West - 1842 - The Chippawa Town Hall is located at the intersection of Main Street and Cummington Square in the former village of Chippawa. It is an example of simplified Greek Revival storefront architecture. The lower story façade is evenly divided by four plain pilasters with simplified Doric capitals. The cream-colored clock tower is visible over many of the other buildings in the area. The expensive granite façade is a surface facing, while the structure underneath and on the side façade are composed of a yellowish-grey coursed rubble stone found in the Niagara peninsula and often associated with the buildings in the Falls area.

After 1851, the general store building was used as a town hall with the lower floor rented to tenants in the grocery and dry goods trade. Part of the space upstairs was rented out for dances, church benefit shows, religious plays, travelling shows with minstrels and local civic association meetings. The remaining area was used to conduct political business for the town.

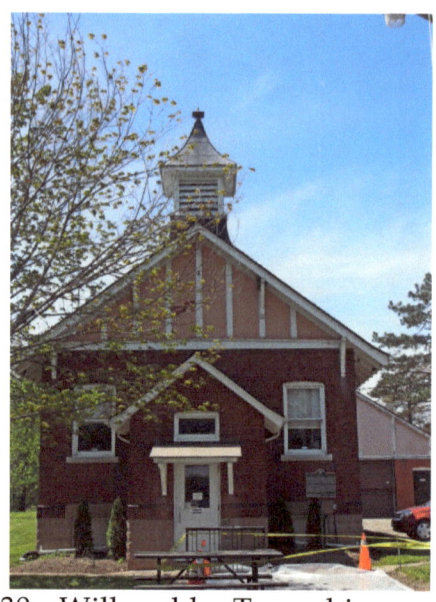

   In the 1830s, Willoughby Township was divided into seven school sections. School Section 2 served those living along the Niagara River. In 1847, a one-room log structure was erected about two kilometers south of here. The school relocated to here and was later replaced by a white frame building during the 1860s. The present brick building was constructed in 1916. The building became a museum in 1968.

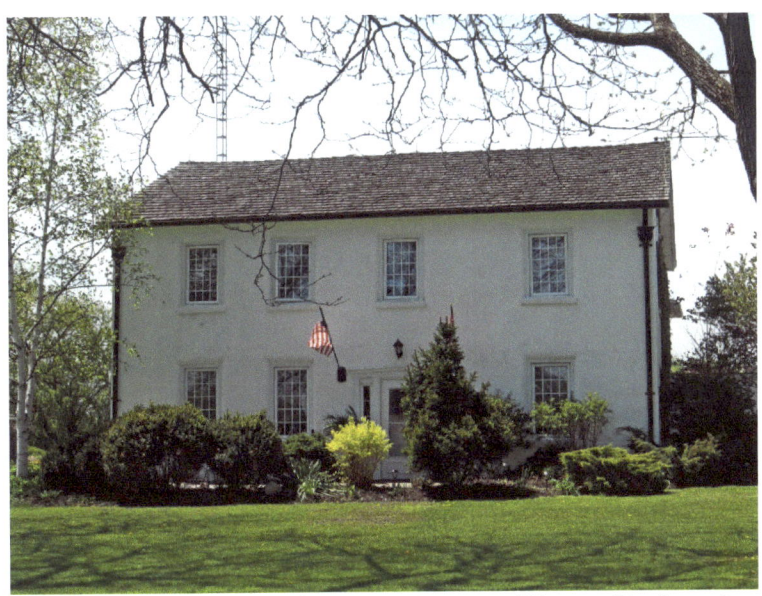

12549 Niagara Parkway – Danner House Bed and Breakfast – It was built in 1805 by American immigrant Ulrich Strickler, after moving from Pennsylvania in 1801. It is a stone building with a stucco finish in an early Loyalist Georgian style. The Danner-Sherk House is a solid construction of stone with a white stucco finish, four irregularly spaced bays across the front and a low pitched roof. The house has the original front entry including the side lights, six-panel door and wood paneling in the door recess.

During the War of 1812, his crops and supplies were taken by American troops leaving him with little for survival. Later the house was occupied by the British. After the war in 1816, the house was sold to Joseph Danner, a Quaker from Pennsylvania who moved to Canada in 1807. Danner owned the property from 1816 until 1847; during this period he reconstructed sections of the home and continued to farm the land. The house was again occupied by troops during the 1837-1838 rebellion as were most homes during this time.

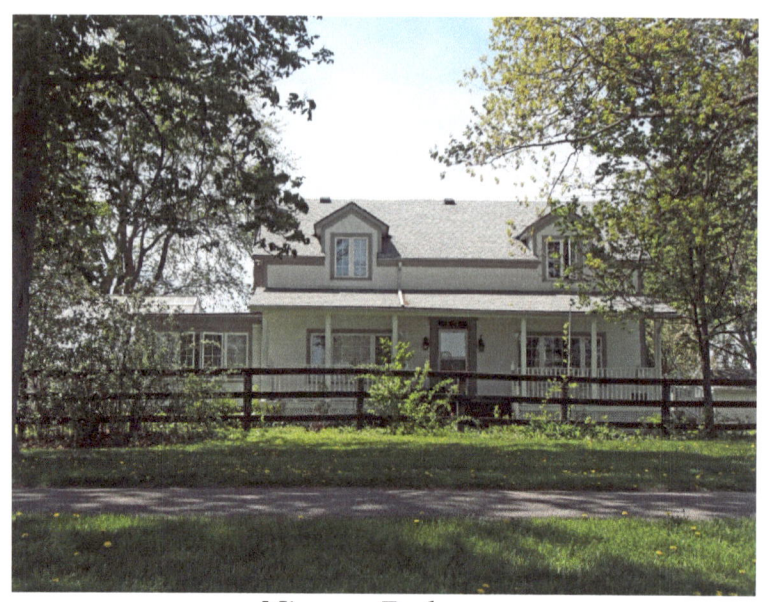

Niagara Parkway

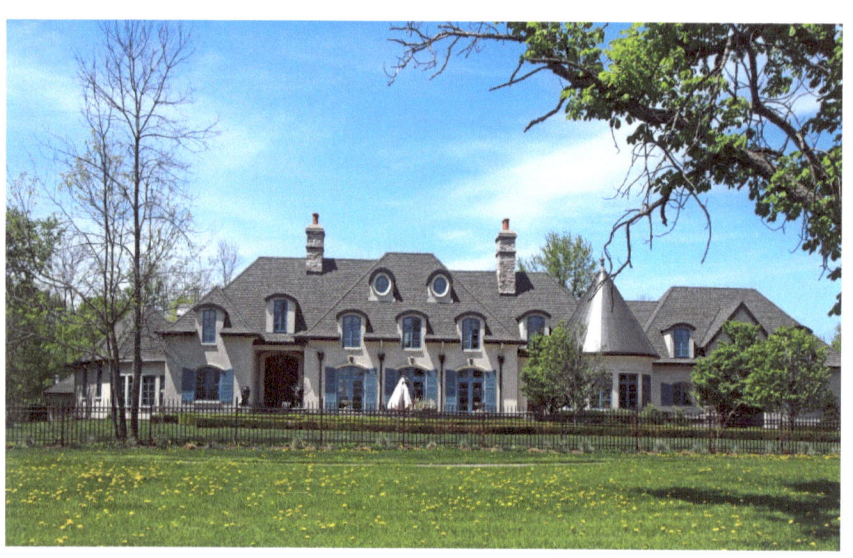

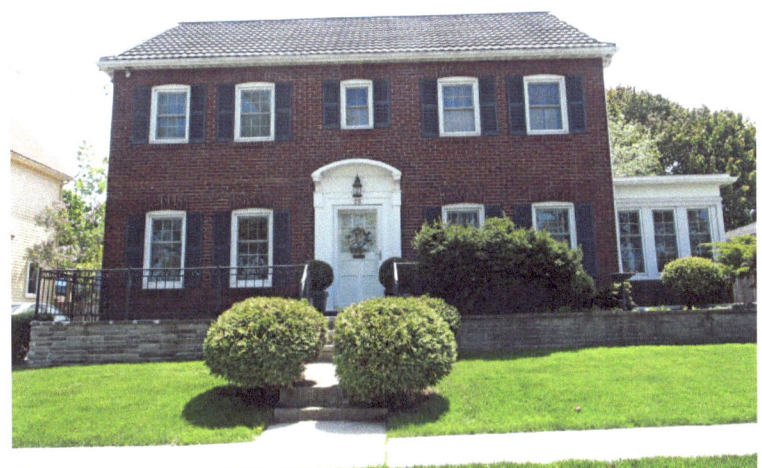

25 Bowen Road

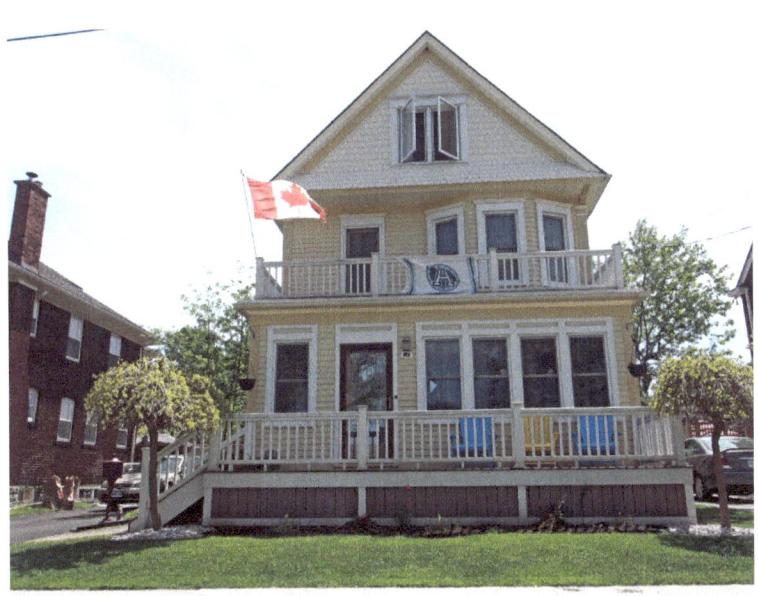

21 Bowen Road

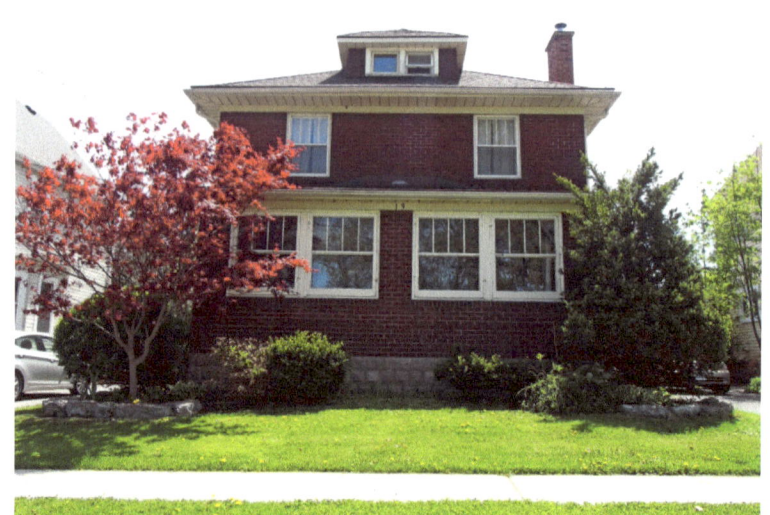

19 Bowen Road

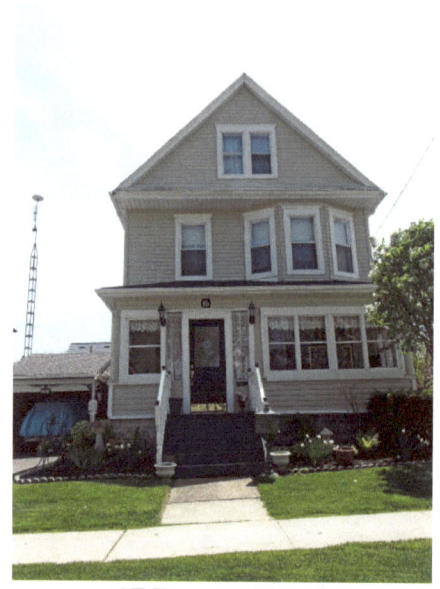

17 Bowen Road

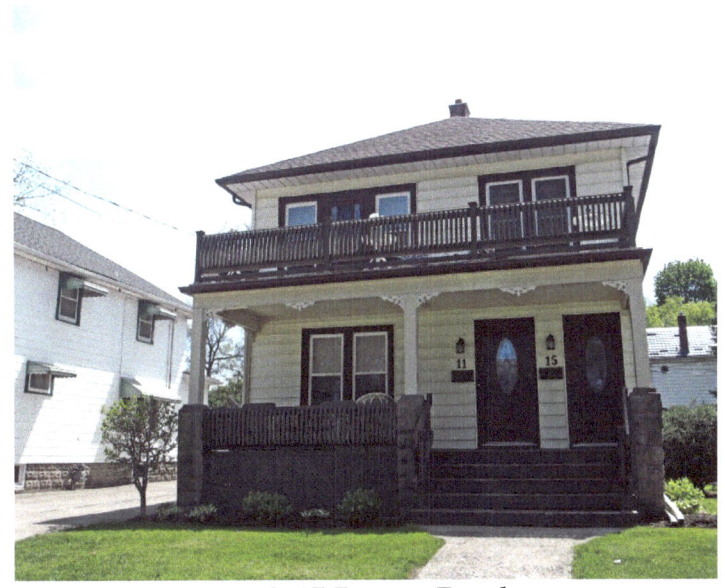

11 & 15 Bowen Road

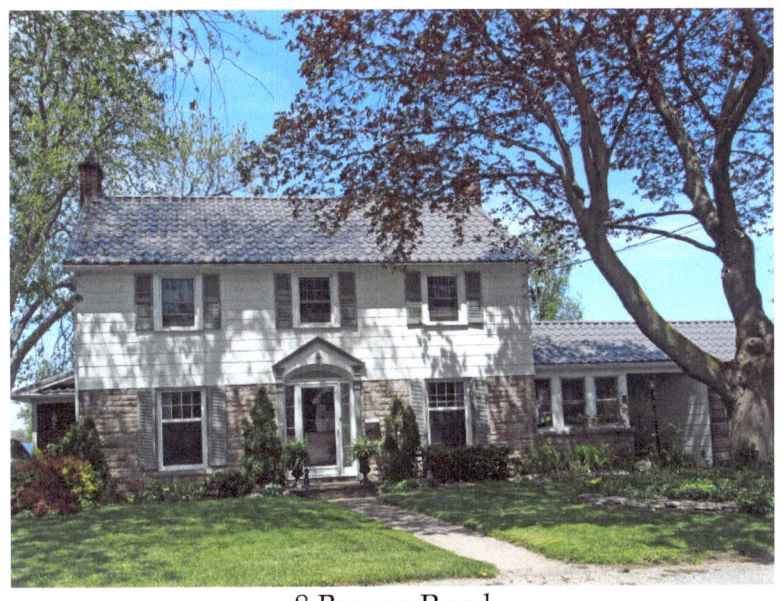

8 Bowen Road

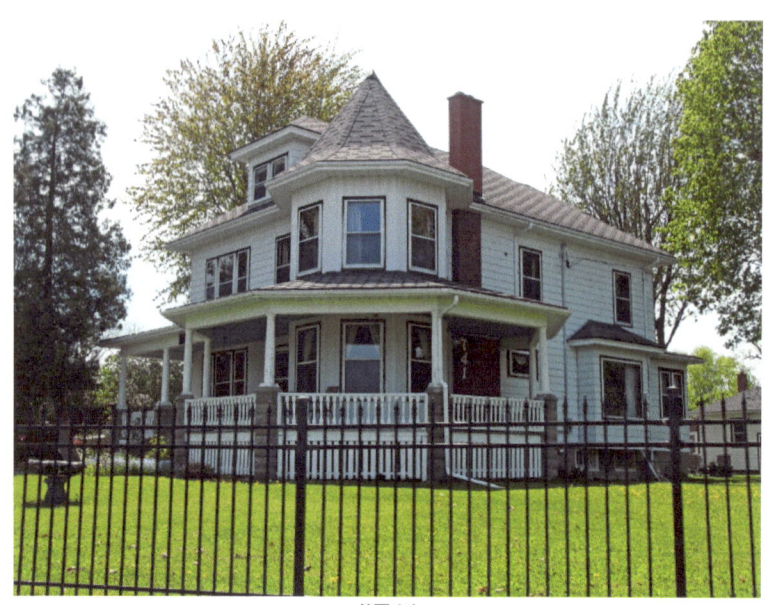

#741

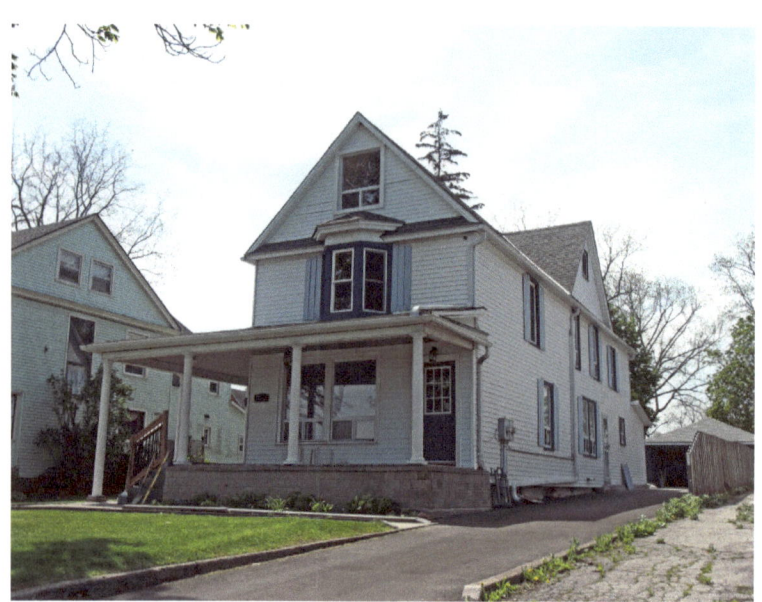

#707

Building Styles

Classical Revival, 1820-1860 – This style was an analytical, scientific, and dogmatic revival based on intensive studies of Greek and Roman buildings, concerned with the application of Greek plans and proportions to civic buildings. Schools, libraries, government offices, and most other civic buildings were built in the Classical Revival style. The white columned porches of the Classical Revival domestic buildings are identified with the mansions of wealthy land owners in Canada.

Georgian, before 1860 – This style began with the British King Georges in the 18th century. These buildings have balanced facades around a central door, medium-pitched gable roofs, and small paned windows.

Gothic Revival, 1830-1890 – These decorative buildings have sharply-pitched gables with highly detailed verge boards, pointed-arch window openings, and dichromatic brickwork. It is a common style in Ontario.

Greek Revival – have gabled or hipped roofs with low pitches. The cornice of the main roof usually has a wide band which represents the entablature of classical Greek architecture consisting of the frieze and the architrave. Greek or Roman columns usually support the porch. The front door is surrounded by sidelights and a rectangular transom and is usually dressed with pilasters, pediments and/or columns.

Italianate, 1850-1900 – A two story rectangular building with a mild hip roof, a projecting frontispiece, and generous eaves with ornate cornice brackets was the basis of the style; often there are large sash windows, quoins, ornate detailing on the windows, belvederes and wraparound verandahs. Italianate commercial buildings often have cast iron cresting and elegant window surrounds.

A **log cabin**, built from logs, was usually one- or 1½-storys constructed with round rather than hewn, or hand-worked, logs, and erected quickly for frontier shelter. Log cabins were built from logs laid horizontally and interlocked on the ends with notches. The cabin was situated to provide sunlight and drainage so the pioneers could cope better with the rigors of frontier life. The pioneers chose old-growth trees that were straight and had few knots and did not need to be hewn to fit well together. Careful notching minimized the size of the gap between the logs and reduced the amount of chinking with sticks and rocks or daubing with mud to fill the gap. The length of one log was the length of one wall.

Loyalist style - Timber frame houses with clapboard exterior finishing. In the Loyalist house, the dining room had a fixed position and had particular interior moldings, curtains and detailing to suit it. Fluted pilasters, a large cornice and a plain but prominent architrave were distinct elements of the Loyalist window surround.

Neo-Classical, 1810-1850 – This style was a direct result of the War of 1812. Many Upper Canadians returning from the war with the United States were second or third generation Loyalists who had inherited land and means from their forefathers. Once the conflict had passed, they had the money and the time to expand their holdings and indulge their architectural whims. Both residential and commercial buildings were constructed on the traditional Georgian plan, but they had a new gaiety and light-heartedness. Detailing became more refined, delicate, and elegant.

Neo-Colonial (also Colonial Revival, Georgian Revival or Neo-Georgian) architecture seeks to revive elements of architectural style of American colonial architecture of the period around the Revolutionary War which drew strongly from Georgian architecture of Great Britain. Architecture from the 18th and early 19th centuries in Ontario includes a wide assortment of detailing and ornament applied to a design centered around the fireplace and the source of water. Structures are typically two stories, have a symmetrical front facade with elaborate front doorways, often with decorative crown pediments, fanlights, and sidelights, symmetrical windows flanking the front entrance, often in pairs or threes, and columned porches.

Regency Style, 1811-1820: Numerous towns and cities enjoy elegant rows of terraced houses built in what is now called the Regency Style. Windows are tall and thin, with very small glazing bars separating the panes of glass. Balconies are of extremely fine ironwork, made of such delicate curves as to seem almost too frail to support the structure. Proportions are kept simple, relying on clean, classical lines for effect rather than decorative touches. Windows and doors, particularly those on the ground floors, are often round-headed. Curved bow windows are popular, and detached villas often featured garden windows extending right down to the ground.

Tudor Revival – exposed timbers with stucco infill, multi-paned windows.

Vernacular/Traditional Mode 1638 - 1950
Influenced but not defined by a particular style, vernacular buildings are made from easily available materials and exhibit local design characteristics.

Other Books by Barbara Raue

Coins of Gold
Arrows, Indians and Love
The Life and Times of Barbara
The Cromwell Family Book
Laura Secord Discovered
Daddy Where Are You?

Montana Series
Book 1: Montana Dream
Book 2: Life on the Montana Frontier
Book 3: Montana to Boston and Back
Book 4: Montana Sons Go to War
Book 5: Montana Sons Return from War

Donaldson Series
Book 1: Rite of Passage
Book 2: Rite of Marriage

Barbara is The Authority on Saving Our History One Photo at a Time. She is pursuing her interest in photography and architecture by preserving a record through photos of old buildings from the 1800s and 1900s with their unique architecture. Enjoy the beautiful architecture in the comfort of your living room. Dream about what it was like in those bygone days. Dream about what it was like to live in a mansion like one of those in this book.

Barbara Raue, a wife, mother and grandmother, is an avid reader and writer. She has researched and compiled several family histories. In 2010, Barbara published her book "Coins of Gold," which celebrates the courageous life of her mother, May Todd. Barbara's second book is a historical fiction "Arrows, Indians and Love" which takes place in Boonesborough, Kentucky during the time of Daniel Boone. In 2013, Barbara published *The Cromwell Family Book* in which she traces her ancestry generations back into Great Britain. Her second novel is called *Laura Secord Discovered*, in which the story of Laura's service during the War of 1812 is shared. Barbara's memoir is titled *Daddy Where Are You?* It tells of her life growing up without a father. Five novels in the Montana Series have been published, *Montana Dream, Life on the Montana Frontier, Montana to Boston and Back, Montana Sons Go to War*, and *Montana Sons Return from War*. The Donaldson series of two novels is available: *Rite of Passage* and *Rite of Marriage*.

This is a link to Barbara's website to view all of her books
http://barbararaue.ca

www.ingramcontent.com/pod-product-compliance
Lightning Source LLC
Chambersburg PA
CBHW040226220526
45473CB00001B/134